HAVING BRUNCH
with GOD

Weekly Devotionals That Provide
Spiritual Nourishment

CONONIAH M. MCCARTHY

WESTBOW
PRESS®
A DIVISION OF THOMAS NELSON
& ZONDERVAN

WestBow Press books may be ordered through booksellers or by contacting:

WestBow Press
A Division of Thomas Nelson & Zondervan
1663 Liberty Drive
Bloomington, IN 47403
www.westbowpress.com
844-714-3454

ISBN: 978-1-6642-7770-0 (sc)
ISBN: 978-1-6642-7771-7 (hc)
ISBN: 978-1-6642-7769-4 (e)

Library of Congress Control Number: 2022916710

Print information available on the last page.

WestBow Press rev. date: 10/11/2022

To my parents the Late Charlesworth Ishchayil McCarthy and Patience Elaine McCarthy who have been instrumental in setting a foundation, from my youth, to serve God.

To my loving wife Andrea McCarthy and my daughter Aniyah McCarthy, for their patience and support during my dedication to this work. This book would not be possible without you.

To the Creator of all things, Adonai, who have provided life, and the resources to make this work possible. And to His mercy towards me; He has allowed me to work in His ministry.

CONTENTS

INTRODUCTION

This weekly devotional is geared towards inspiring a closer connection with God amid a dark world. This world is dark with so much terror, disaster, sickness, and injustice. Given the darkness of this world, we can succumb to focusing more on darkness than we do on the light. But, focusing more on the light instead of the dark allows us to have a more fulfilling and satisfying life. Who is the light you ask? The light is none other than God's son Yeshua, who you may also know as Jesus.

In this devotional, you will see the name Yeshua is used to connect you to the Hebrew text. The original name for God's son is Yeshua. Additionally, you may see words like Adonai, the Hebrew translation for the title Lord. And you will also see YHWH or Yahweh, referring to the true name for God.

We all value the names we are called; it identifies who we are. Similarly, when we appreciate and call-out the original names of God and His son, we are showing God and His son how much we value them. Therefore, the Hebrew names are referenced throughout this devotional.

Beyond the Hebrew names, spiritual concepts will be discussed that lean into the Hebraic understanding of God's word. Understanding the bible from the Hebraic perspective will allow us to unearth the colorful thoughts and meanings behind God's word, this is how we can really bring to life the word of God.

Another important nugget about this book are the weekly topics. As the title suggests, Having Brunch with God is truly about looking at situations or statements in a brunch venue that deduce a spiritual message for the believer in today's world. For example, a week's devotional topic titled "Please wait to be seated" unsheathes the message of obedience. The message of obedience is the lesson for us to learn to be humble enough to subject ourselves to God's ultimate will and authority. Submitting to God's authority, by extension, means humbling ourselves to the authority God has placed over us.

Another biblical lesson that could be derived from the sign "Please wait to be seated," is the lesson on patience. Sure, we would all like to get to the venue then sit immediately, then be served at once. But here we are reminded of God's words, "those who wait upon the Lord shall have their strength renewed."

Now, in tandem with the spiritual messages behind brunch situations, I share my professional and personal experiences. This helps to set the stage for a pragmatic connection between life and God's word. In reality, whenever we are in food settings, like brunch, we talk and share experiences about relationships, family, work, and school. So, the experiences used in this devotional exemplifies that reality and makes God's word comprehensible to everyone.

Finally, this weekly devotional does not stop at expounding on the spiritual messages behind brunch situations or the sharing of personal experiences. This devotional lays out practical exercises and prayers that you can engage in to walk out your faith.

Now that you have an idea of what to expect, my prayer is that this devotional connects you closer to God, supports your spiritual journey, increases your faith, and that you experience new blessings directly from the Father's hands.

"THANK YOU FOR JOINING US FOR BRUNCH!"

The Spiritual Message: Learn to be thankful.

It is Monday morning, your alarm signals it is time to jump out of bed, get dressed, and proceed to work knowing your busy day will include a barrage of spreadsheets, PowerPoints, complaining colleagues or a difficult boss. Just the thought of going through this cycle again brings stress to your mind. Some folks begin to wonder why they haven't retired, or they begin to question their career choices. Some might fantasize about calling in sick for the day. Sounds familiar? We, I think, have all been guilty of this at some point. Let's reflect.

Think about your friends that lost their jobs over the last few months. Think about how many homeless individuals you pass on the road. Or better yet, think about the fact that there are people in the world that went to sleep on Sunday night that did not make it to Monday morning. They will not get to say I love you to family, they will not make it to their favorite coffee shop, they will not make it to the conference room to make that significant presentation.

The point is we should always remember to start our day giving thanks to God, because life could be worse than it is. Give thanks that you are alive. Give thanks that you have another opportunity to live out His purpose for you. Remember the words of King David

"Oh give thanks to the Lord, for He is good! For His mercy endures forever." (*New King James Version,* 1 Chron. 16.34).

The word *thanks*, I believe, has great power to it. The Hebrew word for *thanks,* used in 1 Chron. 16:34, is *yadah (יָדָה). Yadah,* in its practical form, means to extend or hold out your hands – portraying a form of reverence.

Giving thanks is amplified even more once you look at the Hebrew letters in the word *yadah (יָדָה),* then examine their ancient picture representation. The Hebrew word *yadah* comprises three Hebrew letters: *Yud, Dalet* and *Hey. Yud* (יָ) – represents an arm, *Dalet* (דָ) – is a door/movement, *Hey* (הָ) – is a man with arms raised. When we put this altogether you get the image - *hands, breaking through doors with arms raised.* In other words, giving thanks is a powerful full body experience that mirrors rejoicing, it's not just a verbal comment.

The ability to give thanks, despite not having the perfect career or working at the perfect place, may very well open the opportunity for you to break through new doors and experience greatness. God will reward you for your attitude of gratitude.

I will close with this, remember Paul's message to the congregation in Thessalonica "Always be joyful. Pray regularly. In everything give thanks, for this is what God wants from you who are united with the Messiah Yeshua" (*Complete Jewish Bible*, 1 Thess. 5.16-18). Meditate on these words, stay thankful, and stay rejoicing. As you jump out of bed in the mornings, remember, give thanks! Walk out knowing you can be thankful despite of everything.

WEEK 1 | ACTIVITY

List 10 things you plan to be more grateful for over the course of the upcoming week. Be intentional to memorialize the list, then make a conscious effort to be aware of how you have changed your mindset about these 10 things. Revisit this list 3 months later to reflect on how your life has changed since your adjustment on gratitude.

_____

_____

_____

_____

_____

_____

_____

_____

_____

_____

_____

_____

_____

_____

2

WEEK

"ARE WE THE ONLY ONES WAITING IN LINE?"

The Spiritual Message: It's ok to be different.

As you climb the ladder in your place of employment, you will hear from mentors and communication trainings a valued business dictum: "Be Brief, Be Bright, Be Gone." The crux of this statement is that it challenges the consummate professional to be impactful when communicating to executives in an organization. Executives' time are intensely occupied, consequently the abbreviated time you have with them should be 1) Concise - avoid an elongated speech that has minimal value 2) Strategic - present the three main ideas you need to relay 3) Impactful – realize less is more; say what you need to say but create the opportunity for a follow-up. All these variables are great tidbits that even the faith-based professional should adapt and execute in the workplace.

But of course, my focus isn't on providing a business lesson. As believers, our ministry requires us to go a step further than the business dictum "Be Brief, Be Bright, Be Gone." Our ministry calls for us to "Be Brief, Be Bright, and Be Different." Yes, be different! And I am not talking about the proverbial business concept of standing out because of a nice suit, or a well-designed presentation. I am referring to the spiritual concept that if we are a child of God our ways must be different than that of our non-believing friends and colleagues.

What does it mean to be different? To be different means to be holy. Most individuals have an abstract understanding of being holy. Some relate holiness to a high-level of piety or to degrees of self-deprivation. The word is not as opaque as we think. When you review the scriptures, the Hebrew word used in the Bible is *qadosh*. The word *qadosh* means to be set apart. Leviticus 20:26 reads "You are to be holy to me because I, the Lord, am holy, and I have set you apart from the nations to be my own" (*New International Version*). Said another way, "You are to be set apart (different) because I, YHWH (The Lord) am also set apart (different)."

If you understand the context of Leviticus 20 you will garner a greater appreciation for being different. Here is the context, the children of Israel were journeying to the Promised Land, but the land that they were getting was occupied by nations that were the complete antithesis of God. These nations practiced human sacrifices, sexual immorality, witchcraft, and other detestable acts. Therefore, in Leviticus chapter 20, God told His people to be different and not be like those who do not know nor serve Him. This is the same message for all believers today: be different.

We are children of God, right? Then if we are, we are reminded to act accordingly. One of my favorite words from Yeshua are " …Let your light shine before others, that they may see your good deeds and glorify your Father in heaven" (*New International Version*, Matt. 5.16).

Every time we are out in the world, we are representing the God brand. The things we say, the way we dress, our behavior to our supervisors, our water cooler conversations with our colleagues, these all impact the way others perceive us and our creator.

Here are good questions to ask ourselves, can others tell me apart from non-believers? Do I act set apart? Do I act different? Imagine, if your spiritual leader (i.e., rabbi, pastor, priest or elder) was to unexpectedly show up at your workplace tomorrow, or call your employer, how would that experience go? If your spiritual leader loudly proclaimed that they were looking for their devoted congregation member, how would that scene unfold. Would your coworkers' eyes pop as they murmur to each other? Would they smile and say to themselves no wonder Jane acts the way she does, or Joe acts the way he does?

Being holy at our places of worship is expected. But, being set apart or different when we are away from our building of worship is what Yeshua wants for us as stewards of His ministry.

Do the things that will set you apart as a believer so others will be able to say she/he is different, then they will be drawn to the Father!

WEEK 2 | ACTIVITY

Recollect the experiences you have had over the past six months, which of those experiences in retrospect should have been managed differently so that God could have been better magnified in the situation. List the experiences you can remember, then note how you would address the situation differently if faced with a similar situation in the future.

_____

_____

_____

_____

_____

_____

_____

_____

_____

_____

_____

_____

_____

_____

3

"LET'S BLESS THIS MEAL."

The Spiritual Message: Prayer is your formula for success.

How do you start your day? Is your first action to turn and check your work email, Instagram, or your Facebook page? Once you have another chance at life prayer should be your first action to start your morning. Prayer must be a vital part of a believer's daily routine, not limited to just Saturday or Sunday.

With so much to do, I know sometimes we feel as though it is impossible to take a little time to pray. However, our feelings are wrong. You see, with the demands of life we cannot afford to NOT take time to pray. Prayer is our communication line to our Father. It is necessary that we prep ourselves for all that the day entails by seeking God's help to deal with that difficult supervisor, that unpleasant coworker, or just to be granted the courage to overcome that seemingly difficult assignment that stands as a hurdle.

Do not be afraid to go before God; do not worry about the words to say. The way that you voice your problems or concerns to your spouse or family is the same way you can voice the concerns on your heart to God. Even before we utter a word God already knows the issues we deal with (*King James Version*, Ps. 139:4). This is not a license to avoid prayer, but to provide the comfort you need to be willing to go to God. Based on Psalms 139 you can now find solace in the fact that He is waiting to hear from you – your prayers can yield results!

I want you to observe this trend seen in the scriptures. First, let's look at Exodus 2:23:

> And it came to pass in process of time, that the king of Egypt died: and the children of Israel sighed by reason of the bondage, and they cried, and their cry came up unto God by reason of the bondage (*KJV*).

Second, let's look at 2 Samuel 22:7:

> In my distress I called upon the Lord and cried to my God: and he did hear my voice out of his temple, and my cry did enter into his ears (*KJV*).

Do you notice a common theme in the two verses listed above? The common theme is the effectiveness of a believer's cry in their prayers. Realize this, prayer provides the vulnerability and humility you should rightfully show before God. In your complete meekness when you pour out your heart before God and begin to cry out your needs and cares before him, your prayers are most powerful then. Whenever the children of Israel or David cried out before God the text tells us their cries moved up to heaven, directly to the ears of God. To me this is powerful in understanding the authority God has given us, His servants, to overcome the hurdles we have before us. You may wonder, doesn't He know what we are going through? Yes, He knows what we are going through, but like any other loving relationship, communication is key. God wants us to be vulnerable and pray, crying out our needs to Him, then our cries will rise to heaven like incense, and He who is all mighty and powerful will hearken unto us and deliver us from all our troubles.

Hopefully, you realize that choosing to not pray is essentially relinquishing the power you possess. Start your day off right by centering your heart, mind, and soul on your personal communication with God through prayer in the mornings. The secular matters of this world can and should wait while you prepare yourself for the day's challenges. Whatever challenge arise, understand that your morning prayer is the formula to overcome that challenge!

WEEK 3 | ACTIVITY

List all the things you need God's urgent intervention in, then over the next seven days carve out a time to pray specifically for these needs every day. Place on your calendar, either electronic or non-electronic, a special time of prayer. During this dedicated prayer time, be vulnerable and cry out to God over these needs.

_____

_____

_____

_____

_____

_____

_____

_____

_____

_____

_____

_____

_____

4

"GREAT MEAL, LET'S DO ANOTHER PRAYER TO CLOSE."

The Spiritual Message: Pray, then pray, then pray again!

$\mathscr{O}$k, so you have made the commitment to carve out time on your busy schedule to pray for specific areas you need God's deliverance in. I am sure you have already seen the change in your life by the mere fact you have enforced the spiritual power that God has granted you. The fact of the matter is the more you communicate to God the more power you are igniting for full deliverance for any hurdle you are facing. So, is praying one time in the day enough? Here is the thing, you can pray as many times a day as you wish. Our creator has no cap on how many prayers and cries that can be sent up to him. There is no angel screening our prayers then returning them to us void because we met the quota for the day. I believe, based on the evidence in scripture, there is significance in praying at least three times a day.

Our first example is Daniel. Daniel prayed three times a day amid danger:

> Now when Daniel knew that the writing was signed,
> he went into his house; and his windows being open
> in his chamber toward Jerusalem, he kneeled upon his

knees three times a day, and prayed, and gave thanks
before his God, as he did aforetime *(KJV,* Dan 6:10*).*

Daniel showed that he would be unwavering to his faith even
though a decree was made that would jeopardize his life; he still
carried out his usual three prayers a day to God.

King David is our second example, he too prayed three times
a day:

Evening, and morning, and at noon, will I pray, and cry
aloud: and he shall hear my voice (*KJV,* Psalms 55:17).

This is a great example for us because we know David was truly
a man after God's own heart. But we should also ask about Yeshua
and his talmidim (disciples), did they pray three times a day as well?
Well from the recount in Acts we have evidence that the disciples
prayed at the third, sixth and ninth hour. See Acts 2:15, Acts 10:9
and Acts 10:30. During the time of the Messiah the third hour was 9
a.m, the sixth hour was noon, and the ninth hour was 3 p.m. We also
see that in Acts 3:1 the disciples observed the usual time of prayers:
"Now Peter and John went up together into the temple at the hour of
prayer, being the ninth hour" (KJV). It was common practice in first
century Judaism for Israelites to pray three times a day following the
examples from Daniel and King David.

A final note we should consider is the scriptural significance of
three. In scripture, whenever you see the number three, it refers to
life or death. Here are a few examples:

A reference to life:
And there they were with David three days, eating
and drinking: for their brethren had prepared for them
(*KJV,* 1 Chronicles 12:39).

A reference to death:
For as Jonah was three days and three nights in the whale's belly; so shall the Son of man be three days and three nights in the heart of the earth (*KJV*, Matthew 12:40).

A reference to life:
Yet within three days shall Pharaoh lift up thine head, and restore thee unto thy place, and thou shalt deliver Pharaoh's cup into his hand, after the former manner when thou wast his butler (*KJV*, Genesis 40:13).

The takeaway from this is knowing the significance of three is also a connection to life! I believe praying three times a day was not a mere coincidence by the forefathers of our faith; I believe committing to pray at least three times a day can yield your life great dividends, enough to help you usurp the greatest life obstacles. I know you may be busy with a demanding schedule but find the time to spend quality time with God praying life into those seemingly hopeless situations. Whatever problem you are facing today is minuscule compared to His grandiose power!

WEEK 4 | ACTIVITY

Over the next three weeks make the effort to pray three times each day. Worry less about what you will say and just treat that special time as a moment for your one-on-one time with God. Be intentional and list the three times in the day you will be connecting with God.

_____

_____

_____

_____

_____

_____

_____

_____

_____

_____

_____

_____

_____

5

WEEK

"CAN YOU ADD COFFEE, I'M SO TIRED FROM NO REST."

The Spiritual Message: You have a Sabbath, use it!

"*By* the seventh day God completed His work which He had done, and He rested on the seventh day from all His work which He had done" (*New American Standard Bible,* Genesis 2:1). Our limitless and powerful God created the universe we dwell in over the span of six days, then he found the time to rest on the seventh day. Interesting, isn't it?

Does God really need rest? Of course not! He is all powerful and is not bound by human limitations like mental exhaustion or physical fatigue. For God, the seventh day was more than taking a break from a busy schedule of His new project. So why did He rest on the seventh day? If you read on to verse 3 in Genesis chapter 2 you will garner some insights. The translation in the Complete Jewish Bible (*CJB*) is valuable: "God blessed the seventh day and separated it as holy." The *NASB* uses the word sanctified – "Then God blessed the seventh day and sanctified it …"

In other words, God wanted the seventh day to be different from the previous six days: a set apart day. To make the day holy the Almighty One rested on the seventh day as a vivid example for his creation. The day on its own merit is not holy. The example of the Holy One resting on the seventh day cements the day as holy.

One exegesis of Gen 2:3 is that God knew his creation would need a separated day of rest – a creation that would be mortal, and less powerful than he is, so the Sabbath was created for mankind. Yeshua reminded us of this in Mark 2:27: "Jesus said to them, the Sabbath was made for man, and not man for the Sabbath" (*NASB*). The sabbath is really for you and me.

I know most of us have busy and demanding lives, to the point that taking adequate rest usually appears secondary. But what you must recognize is that in your zeal to achieve more in life you cannot forget the importance of pausing to spiritually connect with your Creator. Physical rest rejuvenates and refreshes you. In this state, you can generate new ideas and develop creative problem-solving solutions. Most importantly, rest allows you to grow spiritually.

Going from workday to workday becomes a cycle that doesn't allow you to pause long enough to meditate on God's word. A day to just meditate on the things of God is the moment you get to be still and hear Him speak to you. How can you hear God without dedicating enough time to be unbothered by work, shopping and all the other distractions the world has to offer? You need a set apart day to meditate and commune with God weekly, just like He commanded.

Obedience to God's word will always provide benefits. Scientific research reported by Inc. Magazine, identified twelve scientific reasons supporting the effectivity of getting a regular complete day of rest weekly. Lower stress, better sleep, overall improvement in health, and a boost in creativity are some of the benefits reported in the scientific research report. The science supports God's word!

Despite how the world portrays the message of constant activity and work, remember that God, from the beginning of time, already approved your weekly time-off! Be faithful! In your obedience to Him you will receive both physical and spiritual blessings.

WEEK 5 | ACTIVITY

If you are not already doing this, this week's activity will be one where you will get to test your personal faith in God. I say this because many individuals would want to provide the reasons why they can't rest. I challenge you to provide the reasons why you can. Let God show up for you on account of your obedience to Him. Over the next three weeks, set aside the seventh day to do no work but just rest and make it your spiritual connection day with God. Sing songs, listen to the Word, listen to music, help others, just unplug from the usual. Try this for at least three weeks, test it, and observe the changes in your life. Over the three-week span, notate the activities you wish to do in your personal time with God, then list the changes you experienced, and the blessings you received. If you are already observing the seventh day as your sabbath, then take the next three weeks to do some introspection. What things do you think you should stop doing so you can bask more in His day of rest? Make note of it and execute over the next three weeks.

_____

_____

_____

_____

_____

_____

_____

_____

6

"I BELIEVE I COULD BE THE GENERAL MANAGER AT THIS RESTAURANT."

The Spiritual Message: True faith is through actions.

*H*ave you been believing for a new job, or praying for a promotion, or seeking to learn something new that's seemingly complex? As a Believer you might have been nurtured to pray consistently for these things. And praying is the right thing to do. But coupled with your prayers and faith should also be action! A passage in the book of James explains this quite well for our understanding:

> What good is it, my brothers, if someone claims to have faith but has no actions to prove it? Is such "faith" able to save him? Suppose a brother or sister is without clothes and daily food, and someone says to him, "Shalom! Keep warm and eat hearty!" without giving him what he needs, what good does it do? Thus, faith by itself, unaccompanied by actions, is dead (*CJB*, Jas. 2.14-16).

James acknowledged that faith and works are different sides of the same coin; faith and works are not mutually exclusive, but they are mutually inclusive. I once heard a minster describe faith as a *sixth sense*. You can touch, smell, taste, hear and see – these are all action-oriented, right? Well then there's faith, the sixth sense. This sense is action-oriented too if you think about it. Real faith entails working towards that thing you are seeking all while doing acts of praying, meditating, and reading His word. While you are executing those acts, God is acknowledging your faith by working on your behalf. He has blessed us with another amazing tool in our arsenal that, once used the right way, is powerful to aid us to attain our goals.

To make this even more practical, think about your current desires for your career. You should ask yourself whether you are doing everything within your range of abilities to get there. I am sure you have met colleagues who complain about not earning enough or feel as though they are always overlooked for a promotion, yet those complaining colleagues arrive at work the latest then leave the earliest. Or those colleagues raise their hands for the trivial tasks but consistently shun the complex assignments. As a people of faith, we should be the complete opposite. We should pray and believe that God will answer our prayers to achieve the growth we desire in our careers and in our lives, but we too must contribute to make that plan complete. It must come with you putting in all effort and work to gain that growth. It may require you learning new things that seem uncomfortable or spending the extra time to plow through intimidating details. Whatever it is you must pray then DO! There is no sense talking about the job you want if you don't create the resume then execute by submitting it to the employer.

In culmination, understand that faith and works are inseparable. Your faith in God for growth and advancement in your career, and life on a whole, also comes with a contribution from you that entails doing. God has already provided the blessing to his children as expressed in Deut. 28:13 – "And the Lord will make you the head and not the tail, and you will only be above, and not be underneath, if you listen to the commandments of the Lord your God which I am commanding you today, to follow them carefully," (*NASB*). But realize the blessing is awarded with the requirement of an action on the part of the believer. Faith without action is dead!

WEEK 6 | ACTIVITY

What are the three major things you have been believing God for? Take a moment to reflect. Have you just idled; you said a prayer but have never done anything to work towards those things you are believing in God for? If so, list those items, then list specific tasks that you will commit to doing over the next month to truly exercise real faith like mentioned in James 2.

_____

_____

_____

_____

_____

_____

_____

_____

_____

_____

_____

_____

_____

WEEK

"THERE'S A NEW ITEM ON THE MENU, BUT I HAVE NEOPHOBIA."

The Spiritual Message: Be strong and courageous God is always with you.

What are you most fearful of in this life? There are numerous surveys that detail common phobias such as the fear of death, major illness, or loosing loved ones. It's interesting to note that the fear of public speaking ranks high on the list of common phobias. The fear of public speaking is referred to as *glossophobia.* According to research, some people fear public speaking even more than death. The Jerry Seinfeld comedic piece sums it up – "To the average person, if you have to go to a funeral, you're better off in the casket than doing the eulogy."

But why are we so fearful of speaking in front of others? If you think about it, it's just one human speaking to a few other humans and speaking some words on a topic everyone was expecting to hear. There are no aliens or scary creatures in the room looking to zap you if you cannot speak their alien language. Yet we fear, why?

Self-consciousness, past failures, discomfort with our bodies, and the concern of judgement from others are a few possible reasons why people fear public speaking. Any one of these reasons may resonate with you. Imagine walking towards the projector to present your latest revenue generating or cost cutting idea, or to bring a word of encouragement to your congregation, or to raise a concern at a public forum, but you are fearful of how others are perceiving you and your ideas. You question whether you are using the right words or if you are dressed appropriately. The universe of thoughts flow through your mind which could ultimately cripple you from being your best. You might be asking, well how can I overcome this or any fear? The short answer is that as a child of God, there is nothing you should fear.

In Exodus 4:10, we see how Moshe (Moses) feels when he was tasked with leading Israel out of Egypt. Moshe's words to Adonai were: "Oh, Adonai, I'm a terrible speaker. I always have been, and I'm no better now, even after you've spoken to your servant! My words come slowly, my tongue moves slowly" (*CJB*).

Here it is folks, Moses, a man that was shown miraculous signs that cemented the power of God was utterly fearful! Before Moses' very eyes God performed miracles, restoring Moses' hands from a leprous state and turning Moses' staff into a snake. Yet that was not enough for Moses to feel confident to speak to the children of Israel. When we read the succeeding text in Exodus 4:11-12 Adonai's response to Moses' fear was "Who gives a person a mouth? Who makes a person dumb or deaf, keen-sighted or blind? Isn't it I, ADONAI? Now, therefore, go; and I will be with your mouth and will teach you what to say" (*CJB*). God's response should have been enough to give Moses the confidence to walk out and do what God asked him to do, instead Moses persisted that God should find someone else.

Moses' human tendencies surfaced, and in this case, his spiritual being was overcome by the shortcomings of his flesh. If Moses was with us today, he would have raised his hand and say I too am fearful to speak because of the judgement of others. The magnitude of the fear to speak publicly is very much amplified in Moses' encounter with God. Despite speaking to God and seeing the wonderous signs, it all got minimized by the giant fear of speaking. Moses is a great example of how we should not react to fear! Instead of being like Moses, be like Joshua instead.

The first chapter in Joshua shares the words "Be strong and

courageous, for you shall give this people possession of the land which I swore to their fathers to give them" (*NASB*, Josh. 1.6-9). These were the words Adonai said to Joshua, and without fear or hesitation Joshua executed the command of God. That command *be strong and courageous* is mentioned five times in the book of Joshua. Five, or *chamesh* in the Hebrew text, is associated with power and strength in the bible. Below are scriptural patterns decrying fear:

1. Five smooth stones were chosen to fight Goliath (CJB, 1 Sam. 17:40) – Five stones selected to overpower and beat the Philistines.
2. Five loaves of bread fed five thousand people – The giving of power and strength to a hungry people.
3. The Torah comprises five books (first five books of the Bible) – The word of God provides daily empowerment.

The scriptural examples emphasize there is no accident the phrase *be strong and courageous* was repeated to the children of Israel five different times in the book of Joshua. Despite the daunting task they had before them God provided the words of encouragement they needed to move forward and conquer the land of Canaan. Fear is your Canaan. Whatever you fear, such as public speaking, fear of flying, or fear of driving, God has given you the power to overcome all fears. God will certainly equip you with the spirit to conquer all your fears so be strong and courageous and you can overcome it!

WEEK 7 | ACTIVITY

What are you afraid of? What fears are like boulders in your life that is stopping you from living out your true purpose? Make a list of your five biggest fears you wish to overcome, then strikethrough every one of them. After doing that say a prayer reaffirming these three statements 1) God is greater than all my fears 2) God has granted me the ability, as His child, to overcome all fears and 3) I will be strong and courageous this day forward to conquer all fears before me. After engaging in this exercise, choose a fear to focus on for a week. Find opportunities to engage the fear you are focusing on and write down what you did to face the fear and how you felt before, during, and after each encounter. Continue working through a new fear each week until you have completed the list.

I pray you will find yourself less and less gripped by fear. Continue to revisit each fear until you feel you have overcome them.

_____

_____

_____

_____

_____

_____

_____

_____

_____

8

WEEK

"I DON'T THINK YOU SHOULD INSULT THE WAITER."

The Spiritual Message: Be mindful of the things you say.

*S*ay what's on your mind is a common axiom, but is that a good practice? Probably not. The fact is our thoughts should be filtered before words exit our mouths. Words do matter, they can build others up or tear them down. We all learned this in our school years, yet as adults we are often guilty of saying the most hurtful things.

James chapter 3 paints a lucid picture of the might of the human tongue. According to James the tongue is the conduit to tame the wildest of beast on earth, yet the tongue itself is untamable. Think about how often the tongue is used to bless our Creator, then the same tongue is used to curse others that God created. Seems duplicitous right?

James admonishes us against such duplicitous behavior. To guard against such behavior, we must be mindful of the words we speak. We must be mindful of our words while at work, while in our congregations, or even out at the grocery stores. No matter where we are we must guard our tongue.

I think a good lesson for us all is found in King David's words scripted in the Psalms. In Psalms 37:30 we read: "The mouth of the righteous utters wisdom, and his tongue speaks justice" (*ESV*),

Psalms 34:13 tells us: "Keep your tongue from evil and your lips from speaking deceit" (*ESV*), and in Psalms 15 David describes some attributes of a righteous person that sojourns in God's presence. David says the one that will abide with God is the one that " ...does not slander with his tongue and does no evil to his neighbor, nor takes up a reproach against his friend ..." (*ESV*). Is that you? Can you describe yourself as a person who is shining God's light through uplifting words instead of dispiriting words?

One of the common ways we bring down each other in our world today is through slander. But do you know slander is plainly forbidden by God in the bible? Leviticus 19:16 says this:

> You shall not go about as a slanderer among your people; and you are not to jeopardize the life of your neighbor. I am the Lord (*NASB*).

In Leviticus 19:16 it is important to note that the text mentions not to jeopardize life. This is important to note because slander and life jeopardization are connected. Here is how.

Slander is referred to as *lashon hara* in Hebrew, translated as the tongue that is evil. Rabbinic law teaches that when engaging in *lashon hara* several lives are impacted in that one incident: the talebearer, the one who listens, and the one being discussed. The slander that is spread can have financial, social, and even physical ramifications for the victims. In other words, your slander can jeopardize the life of the victim, who could be your neighbor, friend, or colleague.

Growing up I remember kids saying, "sticks and stones may break my bones, but words will never hurt me." How wrong they were! Words in many cases do more harm than sticks and stones. Think about the number of suicide cases that happened because of a rumor or slanderous comment.

The lesson for us is that words matter. Instead of using your words to tear down, use your words to build up. Let your tongue be that instrument that will unearth the note of greatness in someone.

Always strive to be the greatest cheerleader, always seek to motivate others to be better, always be kind with your words. If you do this, I am positive God will bless you as you imitate Him using your tongue to heal instead of pierce.

WEEK 8 | ACTIVITY

Over the next seven days make a conscious effort to be mindful of the words you say. In fact, every day make a note to say something uplifting and encouraging to at least three people. At the end of the seven days, you would have impacted 21 people in a positive way!

Don't forget to write down the experiences when you encouraged folks in the week. How did you feel at the beginning of the journey, and how did you feel at the end of the journey?

_____

_____

_____

_____

_____

_____

_____

_____

_____

_____

_____

_____

_____

_____

"CAN YOU FORGIVE ME FOR SPILLING YOUR DRINK?"

The Spiritual Message: It's the hardest thing to do but forgive.

*Y*eshua is undoubtedly our greatest example of forgiveness. Never has there been an example of a person that showed unmatched compassion to the destitute, by healing, providing, and resurrecting. However, despite all that Yeshua did mankind persecuted him on a tree. And even then, Yeshua said to His Father "forgive them."

Yeshua's words and actions are really the example of benevolent love to an undeserving people. He then taught us to live our lives just like He did. In Luke 6:27-28 Yeshua said:

> Nevertheless, to you who are listening, what I say is this: Love your enemies! Do good to those who hate you, bless those who curse you, pray for those who mistreat you (*CJB*).

What a tough message, Yeshua is telling us that when our enemies hate us, we are to love them instead of returning hate. It's a significant message for us to grasp. But, to understand Yeshua's words even better let's examine what love really means.

The Greek word used for love in Luke 6:27, is *agapao* which means unconditional love; a love given at will without being earned.

This is the same type of love memorialized in verses such as John 3:16:

> For God so loved the world that he gave his only and unique Son, so that everyone who trusts in him may have eternal life, instead of being utterly destroyed (*CJB*).

And similarly in Ephesians 2:4:

> But God is so rich in mercy and loves us with such intense love (*CJB*).

The love spoken of in these passages refer to unconditional love. The unconditional love that God has shown to us as an undeserving people, is the same love that God wants us to show to our neighbors, and to our enemies.

This simple yet seemingly difficult principle is one that I too had to learn. I recall that I once had a colleague, who I considered a close friend. This friend confided in me about a work experience he had. My colleague and friend, who I will refer to as Mark, informed me that his supervisor asked him to do a task. During that task he encountered challenges that drove him to reach out to Joe, another colleague. Joe decided to assist Mark in the exercise. An innocent interaction of colleagues working to help each other turned into an opportunity for betrayal. Mark and Joe shared supervisors, so after the interaction Joe went to their supervisor and besmirched Mark to the supervisor by highlighting Mark's ignorance of the assignment. Joe also emphasized to the supervisor Mark's inability to do basic technical tasks.

When Mark informed me of the betrayal, despite the betrayal was not done to me, I felt hurt about the ordeal. From that moment on I always held contempt in my heart for what Joe did to Mark. But one day, many years after the incident, long after Mark and Joe went on to work for different organizations, Mark with glee in his voice informed me that he communicated with Joe. Mark was so happy to hear of the good happenings in Joe's personal life. When Mark shared his interaction with Joe with me, I was a bit perturbed about why Mark was so gleeful. I said to Mark "do you remember what Joe did to you?" I then went on to help Mark remember how bad a person Joe was. Mark looked at me in amazement and asked, "you remembered that?"

Here I was angry for the sake of my good friend and colleague, treating Joe as an enemy, whereas my friend Mark who was truly the victim was exemplifying the love of Yeshua. Mark was showing true unconditional, undeserving love. In that moment my contempt left me. It hit me that my friend showed to be way more righteous than I was.

To love unconditionally, like God has asked us to, requires us to forgive and let go of the pain and hurt others have caused. Trust me, I know it is hard to simply give this type of love to individuals who appear to be after you, seeking to destroy your name, or seeking to hurt you in some way. But remember this, Yeshua's ask of us is to love our enemies, and do good to them. This is a principle we must grow to accept and practice. Because, after all, even we need God's unconditional love.

WEEK 9 | ACTIVITY

Is there someone that has wronged you and you haven't found the space to forgive them? Here is your time to release that burden of hate that you have been walking around with. You will find it takes way more work to hate than to love.

To begin your journey of release, list the people that you need to offer forgiveness to. List their names and the experience that drove you to withdraw your compassion from them. After making this list I would like you to start the journey of giving forgiveness to these people. Three common steps you can take to release the hate:

1. Pray for shalom (peace) from God
2. Reflect on when someone forgave you, and how that experienced went. What can you draw from that experience?
3. Reflect on the fact that Yeshua saved us and forgives us when we err.

After engaging in the steps above, take the time to call or meet in-person with the person you have held contempt for. Meet with that person then relay to them how they hurt you. Afterwards, inform them of the steps you are taking to release the hate from your heart, let them know you will forgive them. Avoid pushing the conversation into a battlefield rehashing the past and challenging each other on the accuracy of the hurt or blame. Invite a person of faith you trust if you need a mediator or pillar of support. This is a journey that will allow you to grow your relationship with God by offering the heart of love and forgiveness that He has freely offered you.

_____

_____

_____

10

WEEK

"HI! I'M LATE, CAN I GET AHEAD TO PAY MY BILL?"

The Spiritual Message: Be kind to others.

*O*ne of the greatest messages for humanity, given we are usually self-serving, is the importance of kindness. In Ephesians 4:32 Paul writes, "Instead, be kind to each other, tenderhearted; and forgive each other, just as in the Messiah God has also forgiven you" (*CJB*).

Paul's admonition was the direct counter to bitter spirited practices. In an earlier verse, Paul preached "Get rid of all bitterness, rage, anger, violent assertiveness, and slander, along with all spitefulness" (*CJB*, Eph. 4.31). Paul presents kindness and anger as opposing practices for those who are walking in the likeness of God. An unbeliever's practice is loaded with hating and carrying bitterness in their heart. But anyone walking in the paths of God is on the path that entails the spirit of love, the spirit of kindness, and the spirit of compassion.

What I have noticed is that anger, hate, and malice all have one thing in common – they are products of a bitter spirit. The Greek word for bitter used in Ephesians 4:31 is the word *pikria*. Paul used this word bitter (*pikria*) in several of his writings to personify the traits of sin. We see this again in Acts 8:23: "For I perceive that thou art in the gall of bitterness, and in the bond of iniquity" (*KJV*). Anyone living in 60 – 90 C.E., would know the term *gall of bitterness* referred to a poisonous plant. In fact, the term bitterness by an Israelite speaker, which Paul was, connotated poison – poison originating either from a plant or a venomous snake (Lam 3:19, Deu 32:32). Poison destroys, harms, and causes death. Therefore, Paul characterized hate and anger to bitterness (poison) and admonished against being guilty of that spirit.

If bitterness is like poison, ask yourself what happens when you decide to handle poison? Imagine that you are taking an empty bottle and about to attain a toxic poison to hurt someone. Before you can even hurt someone with the poison you first are exposed to the dangers of the poison. You would have to hold the bottle with care, wearing protective gear to shield yourself. What happens if you experience a mishap while handling poison? Before you had the chance to harm someone you would harm yourself first! This is essentially the danger we put ourselves in when we decide to tread down the bitter path of anger, hate, and malice instead of treading down the path of kindness and compassion. In short, don't endanger your peace and salvation by carrying the bottle of bitterness (poison).

To the contrary, if you carry the bottle of compassion and kindness there is no extra burden of protective gear you must carry. If you spill that bottle of kindness, it will fall on you, but you won't get harmed. You will only shore up your salvation and open the door to a bounty of blessings. The CJB translates Proverbs 21:21 as "He who pursues righteousness and kindness finds life, prosperity and honor." This is the message behind practicing kindness – your ability to walk a path that shows compassion to your neighbor and others you encounter sets you up for a blessing!

My challenge to you is to reflect in areas of your life and identify someone you have been unkind to intentionally or unintentionally, then take the step to correct your wrongs. Seek forgiveness then move forward in being kind and compassionate to that person and to others you will encounter in your journey of life. You risk more danger to yourself carrying the bottle of poison called bitterness, than you do carrying the bottle of kindness and compassion.

WEEK 10 | ACTIVITY

In this week's activity you will identify the people or situations that are the reason for harboring bitterness in your heart causing you to be unkind. I guarantee that your life will be even more fulfilling if you accept the opportunity to relieve yourself from the bitterness. List these people and/or situations, not to etch them more into your heart, but list them as a symbolic action that is removing the pain from out of your heart on to this paper. After listing the source of the bitterness say these words of prayer:

> *God, I desire to be the child you want me to be, loving all your people and holding no malice or hate within my heart for the people you have created, for the people you love. I want to let go of all the bitterness in my heart so I can be more like your son Yeshua. Every person and every situation that I have listed on this paper I list before you. Help me to erase the source of bitterness from my heart and replace my bitterness with love and compassion. In the moments when my mind seeks to wonder to the past, may I remember your son Yeshua who has every reason to dislike us for crucifying him; we gave him the most accursed death as an Israelite. Yet he chooses to love on us, interceding daily for us before you Abba. Forgive me for my shortcomings as I release the burden of bitterness today.*
> *Amein.*

_____

_____

_____

_____

11
WEEK

"LOOK AT THE TABLE OVER THERE, DO YOU SEE THAT GUY'S WATCH?"

The Spiritual Message: Ambition is ok, covetousness isn't.

*W*ealth, power, influence, education, fame, all these are facets of the American dream. Some people are blessed to be born with that dream as their reality, many work excessively hard to capture that dream, while others scheme and commit major crimes to temporarily have a hold of that dream. Certainly, there's nothing wrong with desiring more for your life and desiring facets of the American dream. But should we fall into trouble just to achieve these dreams? At what point is our cravings for success pure ambition or covetousness?

Early on in college my dream was simple, from my perspective at least. My dream was to have a loving healthy family, own a home, drive a nice car, and send my children to the best local schools. My goal was to achieve this the only way I knew how –hard work! That was the version of my American dream. So, was that ambition or was that just covetousness?

Well, here is the thing, setting goals to attain the best of life isn't sinful. I know there are some out there that think that a believer that goes after material things is ungodly. But the bible tells us otherwise see Deu 28:2-5:

> If you will do what Adonai your God says: A blessing on you in the city, and a blessing on you in the countryside. A blessing on the fruit of your body, the fruit of your land and the fruit or your livestock — the young of your cattle and flocks. A blessing on your grain-basket and kneading-bowl (*CJB*).

These blessings in Deuteronomy 28 are not intangible, they are physical blessings! The fact that God promises these blessings for those who do His will is showing that He recognizes His people need physical things to thrive while on earth.

However, we can quickly cross over that line to sinning when we focus on materialistic attainment over the attainment of a relationship with God.

When we place jobs, promotions, careers, and success over the things of God we then cross over into idolatry. When we are overcome with the need to have what someone else has, to the point that we purse the things that belongs to another person, then we are in err. That err is covetousness.

The tenth commandment says: "Do not covet your neighbor's house; do not covet your neighbor's wife, his male or female slave, his ox, his donkey or anything that belongs to your neighbor" (*CJB*, Exod. 20.14). Doesn't God's instruction on coveting seems clear? But to assist us in better understanding what covetousness is, let's examine the word.

The Hebrew word for covet is *chamad,* it means to desire. This is the same word used in verses such as Micah 2:2 "They covet fields and seize them; they take over houses as well ..." (*CJB*), Proverbs 12:12 "The wicked covet the loot of evil men, but the root of the righteous gives forth of itself" (*CJB*), and Joshua 7:21: "when I saw there with the spoil a beautiful robe from Shin'ar, five pounds of silver *shekel*s and a one-and-a-quarter-pound wedge of gold, I really wanted them. So I took them. You will find them hidden in the ground inside my tent, with the silver underneath " (*CJB*). These occurrences of covet in the bible reveal that covetousness is really an unrighteous desire for something that belongs to another person.

Now that we have a good understanding of what covetousness is, an additional lesson we should takeaway is that covetousness is also bad because it leads to the sin of idolatry. Idolatry means some thing or being takes the place of God (*CJB*, Deu 17.3). When we covet wealth, fame, career, success and material things and it takes precedent over our connection with God, then we have branded these things as Lord over us.

In closing, keep in mind there's nothing wrong with ambition and seeking the best in life. Having a desire for the things of others and pursuing this to the point it becomes master over you is covetousness, not ambition. Always remember you serve an awesome God that is King of the universe, so as his child, that makes you royalty. Therefore, stay prayerful and God will turn your dreams into reality.

WEEK 11 | ACTIVITY

For what have you been wishing? Take the moment to examine if this dream or desire came to be based on another person's possessions. If you identify such dreams, remove these coveted desires from your heart. Like Abraham, your mission in this world is specific, so too is your blessings. Take the time now to list the things you really desire. Over the next seven days build out a dream sheet. On this dream sheet, list the things you need God's assistance in bringing to fruition. For each desire you have, make an actionable note that will drive you to get closer to your dream, then begin the process to execute. Along with fervent prayer, this will be the beginning of accomplishing the true desires of your heart.

_____

_____

_____

_____

_____

_____

_____

_____

_____

_____

_____

12
WEEK

"I SHOULD GIVE SOME CASH TO THE PERSON SITTING OUTSIDE THE RESTAURANT."

The Spiritual Message: God loves our giving.

$\mathscr{F}$or many of us the value of money was ingrained from a young age; we were told to do chores around the house then we got rewarded with an allowance. These practices were precedents to prepare us for adulthood. You might remember your mother or father encouraging you to fill your piggy bank with coins, just to encourage saving. I certainly remembered my parents teaching me the value of money. I lucidly recall a time when I was putting my socks on a morning before school when I got one of the greatest money lessons of my childhood.

On one bright morning my father, all dressed for work, sat next to me to assist in getting my thin black socks on. During his gracious act to assist me I asked him for a dollar. My request was solely based on the needs of my stomach; I wanted to be like the other kids that walked to the cafeteria to purchase envious meals. As I sat in the chair while he stooped on the floor to assist me with my socks, I asked my father for a dollar. He looked up at me, pulled a dollar out and he said to me, "always remember money is power, do not waste it." I looked at him not sure how to respond, it was truly a simple request from my vantage point, but after his response I felt a mellow situation turned quite complex in a nanosecond. Based on his response, I felt a sense of obligation to not spend that dollar and focus more on the value of saving.

As good as saving sounds for optimal financial management, a financial plan would be incomplete if we do not incorporate tithing. Tithing is our way to say thanks to God for giving us the ability to earn. God is the one that provided the job or the entrepreneurial opportunity that yields the earnings which allows us to maintain a standard living. King David reminds us that "The earth is the LORD's, and the fulness thereof, the world and they that dwell therein" (*21st Century King James Version*, Ps. 24.1-2,). Nothing we have is ours, it's all His. Therefore, the practice of tithing is essentially giving back a portion to God that was really his from the beginning.

If we look at the history of tithing in the scriptures the first occurrence of tithing is found in Genesis 14. Abraham, called Abram at that time, went to war against King Chedorlaomer and his allies so he could rescue his nephew Lot. Abram defeated the enemies, and once victorious, Melchizedek appeared. Abram gave Melchizedek a tithe of everything he and his allies seized from the war. The word tithe in the original Hebrew text is *ma'aser,* this means a tenth, or 10% for more clarity. Abram gave 10% of the loot to Melchizedek, who was described as a priest of God. In additional texts we see further directives on tithing:

> You shall bring there your burnt offerings, your sacrifices, your tithes, the contribution of your hand, your vowed offerings, your voluntary offerings, and the firstborn of your herd and of you flock (*NASB*, Deu 12.6).

In Malachi 3:8 we read that the prophet Malachi condemned the people of God for falling away from God's statutes, he then calls out tithing as an example:

> Would anyone rob God? Yet you are robbing Me! But you say, 'How have we robbed You?' In tithes and offerings (*NASB*).

Our scriptures have given us proof that a good relationship with God requires the giving of tithes and offerings. We can get blindsided believing that our money is just ours because we worked hard for it. Consequently, we avoid giving our hard-earned money away. But here is the thing, if you are a believer praying on your knees for more success in your career, healing in your life, or just deliverance from life's challenges, you cannot afford to not tithe!

To close, I know there are situations in our lives that can make it seem difficult to tithe or give offerings. I challenge us all with the words from Malachi when there are doubts about giving. In Malachi 3:10 it says, "Bring the whole tenth into the storehouse, so that there will be food in my house, and put me to the test, says ADONAI-Tzva'ot (Lord of Hosts). See if I won't open for you the floodgates of heaven and pour out for you a blessing far beyond your needs" (*CJB*).

WEEK 12 | ACTIVITY

Are you giving? If not, here's your time to start. In addition to tithing think about those in your community, whether it's a familiar face or a stranger. Can you think of anyone that needs assistance? Make a list of who those individuals are, then put the foot forward to reach out and offer assistance to them over the course of the next month. This is how we can show God's love, no better way than through charitable actions.

_____

_____

_____

_____

_____

_____

_____

_____

_____

_____

_____

_____

_____

_____

13

WEEK

"WHY WERE YOU AFRAID TO SAY YOU NEVER TRIED THIS DRINK?"

The Spiritual Message: Never be ashamed of God.

$\mathcal{I}$ remember during my days at college there were a band of Muslims that studied together at the university's library. I recalled seeing them rise from their seats, then move to a corner of the library where they then prostrated themselves to the floor. At first, I had no clue what they were doing. After seeing this event repeated over several days, I understood that this event was a daily spiritual experience for them. Seeing this caused me to think introspectively. I pondered on the fact that these young men were praying openly without fear. These men were not worried about their classmates' protrusive stares or perception. These young men were solely focused on engaging in their spiritual experience.

Would you have that type of courage to pray, or share the word of God outside the walls of your place of worship? You might have had those battles where you felt conflicted about sharing the word of God. Your mind shifts into thinking if the place and time is appropriate, or what would others think of you. But the fact is, we cannot be ashamed of the gospel that Yeshua has asked us to share.

In my experience, whenever I felt a sense of refrainment to representing God unapologetically, my mind ran to Luke 9:26:

> For if someone is ashamed of me and of what I say,
> the Son of Man will be ashamed of him when he
> comes in his glory and that of the Father and of the
> holy angels (*CJB*).

These words uttered by Yeshua form the basis for believers to never be ashamed to share the message of God.

Daniel in the bible is a fitting example of someone that was not afraid to stand for righteousness, regardless of the cost. In Daniel chapter 1, we see that Daniel an Israelite understood the teachings of the Torah, the book of instructions and commandments passed down from Moses. Daniel understood the difference between clean and unclean meat and all matters concerning a righteous living. Consequently, Daniel refused to eat the king's food when approached by Ashpenaz, a Babylonian official. Daniel knew the king's food was contrary to God's dietary instructions. Therefore, Daniel refused to eat the king's meat to avoid displeasing God and defiling himself.

Daniel could have easily rationalized why it would have been acceptable to comply with the instructions from the king and not counter the king's orders. But instead, Daniel boldly changed the narrative by seeking to convince the Babylonian official that rather than eating the king's meat he would eat vegetables and stay undefiled.

What's vital in all of this is that Daniel first had the chutzpah to say he would standup for Adonai and do what was right. After Daniel made that decision to choose God, then God intervened by placing a spirit of compassion and favor upon the Babylonian official so that he was submissive to Daniel's request. The lesson, if you make the decision to choose God, He will work out all things for you!

Your willingness to not be afraid or ashamed but to stand for the righteousness of God can be the forerunner to turn around your life, your career, or relationships. There's no need to be fearful or ashamed to share the message of Yeshua.

I will leave you with these words, from Paul to Timothy, which are applicable to us all today: "For God gave us a Spirit who produces not timidity, but power, love, and self-discipline. So don't be ashamed of bearing testimony to our Lord or to me, his prisoner. On the contrary, accept your share in suffering disgrace for the sake of the Good News. God will give you the strength for it" *(CJB,* 2 Tim. 1.7-8).

WEEK 13 | ACTIVITY

Over the next month, start the journey to spread the message of God to someone. There's no scripted way to do this. Share a message with someone in any manner you desire so that one other person in this universe hears the message of salvation. Revisit your journey in a month's time. At the end of the month reflect on the individuals you encountered and how you were able to share the message of God.

_____

_____

_____

_____

_____

_____

_____

_____

_____

_____

_____

_____

_____

_____

14

"HEY, YOU CAN LEAN ON US, WE WILL PAY YOUR BILL."

The Spiritual Message: Your body of believers serve as your refuge.

Most of us have good family members, friends, and colleagues we can complain to about a difficult day or about ongoing issues in our lives. We tend to find refuge in these individuals. These individuals act as supporting pillars to help us ride through the glaring obstacles in our life. This isn't atypical at all. The need for friendship and personal connection is a key need for humans. Maslow's Hierarchy of needs places social connection as the third tier in the hierarchy. After psychological and safety needs are met, humans need to have a base of family or friends for emotional support.

Believe it or not, the Bible endorses the need for this type of support as well. In 1 Corinthians 12:12, Paul writes "For just as the body is one but has many parts; and all the parts of the body, though many, constitute one body; so it is with the Messiah" (*CJB*). Paul is providing the message that the body of believers must regard themselves as one unit like the human body. So how should a unified body operate? Paul explains in verse 26 "Thus if one part suffers, all the parts suffer with it; and if one part is honored, all the parts share its happiness." Paraphrased, if your brother or sister, who is part of the faith, feels hurt, share in their burden and empathize in their situation. Alternatively, if your brother or sister is experiencing great blessings you should rejoice with them.

Paul is emphasizing the need for the believing community to have sound relationships with each other. Believers should be able to confide in other believers regarding their problems or concerns. Believers should be a pillar of support, a place of refuge for others that need help. If we can't run to other believers for help, then who could we run to for refuge? Should we run to the psychic and seers?

In Psalms 46:1 David pens, "God is our refuge and strength, an ever-present help in trouble" (*CJB*). Then again in chapter 62:7 David writes "In God is my salvation and my glory; the rock of my strength, and my refuge, is in God" (*KJV*).

King David is clearly expressing that his place of refuge is in God Almighty. These are two simple *psukim* or verses from the scriptures regarding God as a refuge, but there's more to unravel to reveal the depth of what David was relaying. To fully understand the refuge that we as a body of believers have let's read Numbers 35: 9-15. It reads:

> Then the LORD spoke to Moses, saying, "Speak to the sons of Israel and say to them, 'When you cross the Jordan into the land of Canaan, then you shall select for yourselves cities to be your cities of refuge, so that the one who commits manslaughter by killing a person unintentionally may flee there. The cities shall serve you as a refuge from the avenger, so that the one who commits manslaughter does not die until he stands before the congregation for trial. So the cities which you are to provide shall be six cities of refuge for you. You shall provide three cities across the Jordan, and three cities in the land of Canaan; they are to be cities of refuge. These six cities shall be a refuge for the sons of Israel, for the stranger, and for the foreign resident among them; so that anyone who kills a person unintentionally may flee there (*NASB*).

In simple terms, the cities of refuge were escape towns for any individual that unintentionally murdered someone. This place allowed for the perpetrator to run away to a haven to save his/her life from the avengers. There were six cities spread across Israel, creating enough places for a perpetrator to quickly get to. Rabbinic literature further expounds that the doors to the city were always open, there were legible signs, the road to the city was smooth and clear, and wider than other roads. These variables ensured that perpetrators looking for asylum could escape to the city without interruption. So, we can see here that David, staying consistent with the Hebrew culture of writing in concrete thoughts, was comparing the protection of God to the salvation and protection attained in the city of refuge.

Shouldn't we feel joyous to know that God is our living refuge? Imagine if you just committed this grave accident causing someone to lose their life and you have nowhere to safely hide, no one to explain your case, and no way to be saved. Then imagine yourself following signs leading you to a place of refuge. I am sure you would feel relieved to land in safety out of harm's way. Well, this is what God is for us. When we are downtrodden and broken with nowhere to turn to for help God is that safe place with walls to surround us from the danger that's trying to overtake us.

Therefore, understand that God has created a body of believers for you to be a part of to share in both the good times and bad times. Consequently, identifying God as a refuge involves accepting other believers in your life to provide encouragement, counseling, and prayer support. This is what Paul lauded in 1 Corinthians 12:26.

So, to the original question, who is your refuge? God is our refuge, and He has provided brothers and sisters for us to lean on to aid us through our trials. Whatever you are going through know that you can lean on your brothers and sisters in the faith that can pray with you and provide good biblical wisdom and guidance that you need.

WEEK 14 | ACTIVITY

If you have been shunning a deeper connection with other like-minded believers of the body of Messiah, then this is your moment to take advantage of the benefits of being part of a body of believers. This week's activity is simple. Challenge yourself to:

1. begin attending a place of worship regularly if you haven't previously. This will allow you to draw on the strength of others. We all need this connection, especially when it's within the body of the faithful.
2. Begin connecting to groups in your place of worship. Join with a prayer group, the women or men's fellowship, youth group, or whatever is available.

Challenge yourself to develop a greater spiritual connection to the brothers and sisters in Messiah. You will be surprised how uplifting this experience can be for you.

_____

_____

_____

_____

_____

_____

_____

_____

15

"WHAT WOULD PEOPLE SAY IF THEY SAW ME CRYING HERE?"

The Spiritual Message: Be vulnerable with God.

The word vulnerable usually carries a connotation of weakness. That's because in its most basic form the word vulnerable means to be open to physical or emotional harm. In our daily lives we avoid being vulnerable with others because we do not want to risk the emotional hurt that follows when others disappoint and fail us. But here is the good news we all should hear: God is unlike man; He will not fail us! God is our refuge and strength a very ready help in trouble (*NASB*, Psalms 46.1). Our God and King is unlike those who are failing you now or has failed you in the past. Like the lighthouse that stands unshaken in the stormiest of nights, and the tower which was made with bricks that stands unmoved over the centuries, so much greater is the God that we serve.

You see, being vulnerable to God means placing yourself in those uncomfortable positions as you approach him. For example, removing the pride that you have as you go before his presence. We show humility in His presence when we open our mouth, speak sincerity, admit our short comings then cry out for His help. Don't be afraid of who sees you crying and being vulnerable; you are the one that's going through the struggle and urgently need the deliverance. Being vulnerable with God opens a wide path for your message to get to Him, and it creates the propulsion for Him to intervene on your behalf. Consider these verses which depict people of faith being vulnerable with God:

In Exodus 2:23 we read:

> Now it came about in the course of those many days that the king of Egypt died. And the sons of Israel groaned because of the bondage, and <u>they cried out; and their cry for help because of their bondage ascended to God</u> (*NASB*).

In Numbers, when Miriam was hit with leprosy, what did Moses do to seek healing for her? The text states:

> So, Moses <u>cried out to the Lord</u>, saying, "God, heal her, please!" (*NASB*, Num 12.13).

In Numbers, what were the words Moses recorded? We read:

> But <u>when we cried out to the Lord, He heard our voice</u> and sent an angel, and brought us out from Egypt (*NASB*, Num. 20.16).

In Judges, what did Israel do when they were under persecution and needed deliverance again? The text says:

> But the sons of Israel cried out to the Lord, and the Lord raised up a deliverer for the sons of Israel to set them free, Othniel the son of Kenaz, Caleb's younger brother (*NASB*, Judg. 3.9).

In Samuel, we see the power of vulnerability again:

> Samuel took a nursing lamb and offered it as a whole burnt offering to the Lord; <u>and Samuel cried out to the</u>

LORD for Israel, and the LORD answered him (*NASB,*
1 Sam. 7.9).

There is power in our cries as we are at our most vulnerable.
God wants us to cry out to him. It is through tears we can purge the
problems of our hearts and place it on him. God will take these troubles
and pains we have released then provide the deliverance we cried out
for. I really believe there is so much power rooted in those cries.

The word cry, as used in the bible, is the Hebrew word *tsa'aq*
(קעצ). Hebrew words carry a corresponding picture that aids in
emphasizing their meaning. The corresponding Hebrew pictograph
for the word cry or *tsa'aq* is a trail, an eye, and the sun on the horizon.
This imagery brings out the real meaning behind cry. It describes
your action when you are on a trail, a rocky road. You look up then
look to the hills where the sun sets, seeking His deliverance. This is
ultimately why King David said in Psalms 121, "I will raise my eyes
to the mountains; From where will my help come? My help comes
from the LORD, who made heaven and earth" (*NASB*).

Therefore, I implore you as you face the upcoming days
encountering ebbs and flows in your personal and professional life,
remember to be vulnerable and cry out to God, He promised to
deliver you!

WEEK 15 | ACTIVITY

Israel cried out to God. God heard their cries and delivered them out from Egypt. Is there anything in your life you haven't cried out for, but you desperately need Gods intervention for? This is your time to take another step in your relationship with your Creator. Set aside at least 30 minutes of quiet time over the upcoming week to fall on your knees before God and pray over everything you would like to see God deliver you out of. Cry out over those symbols of Egypt and believe that God will bring you over to a promised path unlike anything you have ever experienced.

_____

_____

_____

_____

_____

_____

_____

_____

_____

_____

_____

_____

_____

16

"FANCY RESTAURANT CHOICE, I SEE YOU HAVE DONE WELL FOR YOURSELF."

The Spiritual Message: Always stay humble.

"Now this man Moshe (Moses) was very humble, more so than anyone on earth" (*CJB*, Num. 12.3). These are the words used to describe one of the most prolific biblical leaders, a man God spoke to face-to-face (*CJB,* Exod. 33.11). There are many successes tied to Moses like, defending the children of Israel before the Egyptians, leading the children of Israel out of Egypt after 400 years of slavery, and delivering the instructions of God and teaching them to Israel. Despite all these accomplishments Moses was humble.

This concept of humility is not one that you will hear pushed a lot in corporate and other professional circles, or the world in general. The world promotes the taunting of accomplishments and self-centricity. If Moses was alive today many in our society would have encouraged him to make self-proclaimed books and probably nudge him to leverage his exodus success for great financial gain. But we just read that Moses was quite the humble man, so a self-absorbing image likely won't fit the Moses we came to know through the scriptures.

If Moses is an example for us believers, then what does it mean to be humble? The world certainly has its own definition, but leaning on biblical principles, we can garner a definition of humble to keep us accountable. The word humble is translated from the Hebrew word *anav* in the scriptures. The word *anav* is evident in the following scriptures:

> For the avenger of blood remembers them, he does not ignore the cry of the <u>afflicted</u> (*CJB*, Ps. 9.12).

> But the <u>meek</u> will inherit the land and delight themselves in abundant peace (*CJB*, Ps. 37.11).

> One who despises his neighbor sins, but one who is gracious to the <u>poor</u> is blessed (*NASB*, Prov. 14.21).

We also see the word humble translated from the Greek *tapeinos* in the New Testament:

> … God is opposed to the proud, but He gives grace to the humble (*NASB*, 1 Pet. 5.5).

> He has brought down rulers from their thrones, and has exalted those who were humble (*NASB*, Luke 1.52).

> Humble yourselves in the presence of the Lord, and He will exalt you (*NASB*, Jas. 4.10).

What can we gather from these texts? Well, we can gather from the text that humble can mean affliction, or even poverty, but these terms are all based on a situation. I think a more utilitarian definition for humble is deprivation of a common resource. When you are poor you are deprived of money and when you are afflicted you are deprived of peace. And when you are regarded as humble in persona, instead of being proud, you have removed the natural behavior of self-absorption. This lowly minded, selfless mentality is what God wants of us. God wants us to be a people that regards others as better than ourselves (*NASB*, Phil. 2:3).

When you look at your personal circle, I am sure you can pinpoint several individuals that regard themselves as higher than others. They taunt their great jobs, careers, car and homes. They boast about things that can quickly dissipate. My encouragement for you today is to shun this natural reaction to appear better than anyone else.

Being humble does not mean that you are self-effacing to the point you allow others to take advantage of you. Absolutely not. Being humble is just indicative of your walk with God; a walk that consists of not boasting despite the great things God has done in your life. Instead, we know living our lives in humility pleases God, in so doing we recognize there's a reward for us. 1 Peter 5:6 guides us to "Therefore humble yourselves under the mighty hand of God, so that He may exalt you at the proper time" (NASB).

I think the additional message for us is to understand that the ultimate glory we seek is that which comes from God. Therefore, if we can carry ourselves as lowly amongst men, then God can raise us up into the blessings He has in store for us in this life, and the next.

In summation, we know that Moses was humble, but Moses was a shadow of Yeshua our Messiah. Yeshua is the greatest example of humility for us all. He left his kingdom of glory and dwelt amongst man on this earth, then He died for us. There is no greater example of humility. As we aim to be more like Him, let's remember to deprive ourselves of the need to appear better than anyone else. May we neglect our pride and have a lowly spirit just like Yeshua!

WEEK 16 | ACTIVITY

As God blesses you and elevates you in this world remember to stay humble; God raises up the lowly and the proud is downtrodden. Knowing this, this week's activity centers on a time of introspection. Focus on how you can be more humble than you have been in the past. If there are areas of your life where you realized you have acted with pride instead of humility, write a few sentences of affirmation. In these sentences, state that going forward you will be more humble by doing specific things (*list the specific things you can do*) or treating others a specific way (*list the specific ways you promise to treat others*). Review these sentences until they carry real meaning in your life.

_____

_____

_____

_____

_____

_____

_____

_____

_____

_____

_____

_____

17

WEEK

"WOW, ALL THIS TIME MY EYES MISSED THE SPECIALS ON THE MENU."

The Spiritual Message: We need God to open our eyes.

$\mathcal{I}$ usually do my best to avoid eating the typical American fast-food diet such as fries, burgers, wings, or pizza. Occasionally my body craves salted fries and seasoned fried chicken. When these cravings become unbearable, I give in and enjoy a treat. I sometimes journey to the reputable Chick-Fil-A to indulge my cravings. Like many, I've glimpsed the Chick-Fil-A logo without paying much attention to it. On one such trip to Chick-Fil-A to indulge my fast-food craving, I sat in the drive-thru chatting with my daughter who was sitting in the back seat. While subconsciously focusing on the logo far longer than usual, I realized the 'C' forms the chicken in the logo, this was so amusing to me. After many years of going to this restaurant I missed this detail, which to some may seem like quite the jovial oversight. So here it is that I looked at that logo for years, viewed it with my own eyes, yet I never realized the imagery and connotation that the logo conveyed.

Maybe you never missed something this glaringly obvious in your life. Maybe you have missed it, but you haven't realized it yet. There may be situations in your life that you need to be unblinded to and acknowledge so you can course correct. Some of these situations we are blinded to may be low or high stakes: jobs, careers, family, or even relationships. Regardless of what they are, to be unblinded we need to pray to God uttering the words "Lord, we want our eyes to be opened" (*NASB*, Matt. 20.33).

We need God's intervention because many times our physical blindness is a product of our spiritual blindness. Let's look at Samson, a judge over Israel for 20 years, who was set-apart by God as a Nazarite for the sole purpose of delivering Israel from the hand of the Philistines. In the end, he made choices that led to a true physical blindness – losing both eyes by way of his Philistine enemies. In Judges 16 we read that Samson was pressed three times by Delilah to provide the secret to his strength. Samson withheld the truth in each incident, but in all those incidents the common theme was that the Philistines came to attack. This seems like a typical script in a movie where we would all watch and shout for the main character to get a clue! How could Samson be so blinded to this? Three times he gave a response to Delilah and all three times the Philistines showed up at his doorstep seeking to capture him. Shouldn't he have realized Delilah was a poison to him and run away from the situation at that point? Shouldn't he have sought after the people of Israel and focus on doing what Adonai had ordained him to do? No, instead Samson did not make the connection like we do now as we recount that story. In the end he couldn't see to comprehend Delilah's ulterior motives; he had no discernment. Ultimately that spiritual blindness led to his eyes being gorged out, so he became physically blind.

Yeshua himself told His disciples that He spoke to the flock in parables because they were a people that were not ready to understand, and so the prophesy of Isaiah would be fulfilled "You will keep on hearing but never understand, and keep on seeing but never perceive, because the heart of this people has become dull — with their ears they barely hear, and their eyes they have closed, so as not to see with their eyes, hear with their ears, understand with their heart, and do t'shuvah (repentance) so that I could heal them" (*CJB,* Matt 13.14-15). The blindness that the flock were experiencing is a blindness that starts with the heart, a blindness that needed to be removed by first submitting wholeheartedly to God's will so that the veil could be removed, and His light revealed.

Paul shares in Ephesians 1:18: "I pray that he will give light to the eyes of your hearts, so that you will understand the hope to which he has called you, what rich glories there are in the inheritance he has promised his people" (*CJB*). The clear vision we need so we can navigate this life and our walk of faith must come ultimately from God.

We are all going through some issue in life that can appear like a major crossroad; we don't know what choice to make. You may be trying to make a life changing decision regarding a relationship you should start or end, or the job you should terminate or pursue, or that commitment you should avoid or engage in. The takeaway is that you should take this time to not rely on your own sight but rely instead on His sight. God is the Aleph Tav, the beginning, and the end, and as such he knows the future – not your psychics or seers. God is not nearsighted like we are, He can provide the spiritual sight you need to be successful in this life. Look to God to provide the spiritual awakening to open your spiritual eyes. He will help you to see and avoid all the plans of the Adversary.

WEEK 17 | ACTIVITY

How can five bible believers read one scripture yet leave with completely different interpretations? Well part of the reason is we are spiritually blinded. We certainly need the Spirit to work in us and reveal the things we should see in His Word so that we can live a more complete life. The one thing we must all recognize is that this spiritual awakening doesn't come upon us magically. We must express the desire to want this. We must express the intent and interest. It is at that point the Spirit will reveal what is seemingly hidden. What are the things in God's Word you are seeking a revelation on? Make today the day when you will commit to applying yourself to the Word of God by committing to search through His word more than you have in the past. I fervently believe by searching out His word more, the Spirit will reveal His truth to you. Then His spiritual revelation will also open your physical eyes to the paths He wants for you in this world.

_____

_____

_____

_____

_____

_____

_____

_____

18

"WHILE WE WAIT FOR DRINKS, TELL ME YOUR NEW PLANS."

The Spiritual Message: Don't let your left hand know what your right hand is doing.

One evening, after toiling through an arduous day of work, I escaped to the sofa, retrieved my personal cell phone, and scrolled through social media platforms eyeing the latest news, comical memes and the storylines from friends and families. While scrolling, I came across a very interesting post from an acquaintance sharing how close they were to becoming a millionaire. The post boasts that, "this is hard work but I'm halfway there," in reference to recent real estate dealings and details on how they are progressing with their ventures. After reading that person's post I pondered why people post such personal information. What could they have been thinking when they wrote that post? Were they attempting to be a pillar of encouragement for those who have dreams? Were they so proud of themselves that they couldn't contain their achievements? Were they hoping to be showered with praise from the world?

I can only guess what they were thinking. The bible, our life instruction manual, makes one thing clear by guiding us with these words from Jeremiah 9:23-24: "This is what the LORD says: Let no wise man boast of his wisdom, nor let the mighty man boast in his might, nor a rich man boast of his riches; but let the one who boasts boast of this, that he understands and knows Me, that I am the LORD who exercises mercy, justice, and righteousness on the earth; for I delight in these things, declares the LORD" (*NASB*).

The social trend of publicly boasting about what we are doing or achieving is quite contrary to the text in Jeremiah 9:23. Yeshua's (Jesus) principle of executing a humble and covert tactic with charity can be applied to all facets of our life – "do not let your left hand know what your right hand is doing" (*NASB*, Matt. 6.3). Said differently, we need to operate below the radar in a way where we do not publicly share and alert every one of our dealings to gain public praise and adoration.

Let's explore this some more by looking at a corporate strategy called **stealth mode**. Stealth mode refers to the phase where a start-up company operates in secrecy as they move from product conception to product launch. Start-ups operate in this stealth mode to avoid unwanted pressures from competitors, preserve intellectual property and cue demand. Ultimately these three benefits of operating in stealth mode tie to one central purpose: to ensure success! When we apply this business principle to our daily lives the result will be the same - we can increase our probability of ensuring success in our relationships, careers, and other aspects of our lives by saying and showing less.

Given this topic, I can't help but think about Yosef (Joseph) as an example of someone that publicly shared his dreams. Joseph shared to his brothers a dream where their bundle of wheat bowed to his bundle of wheat. Joseph's brothers did not receive that dream well. Genesis 37 tells us that Joseph's brothers hated him before the dreams were shared, but they hated Joseph even more after hearing his dreams. Joseph's decision to share his dream, and in greater context allowing the message of his dreams to be divulged, fueled his brothers to ultimately sell him into Egypt. There is a torrent of meanings and lessons we can garner from the Joseph narrative, but in the context of operating in stealth mode, I do believe there is a lesson for us all on managing what we say and when we say it.

God has revealed in His word that when we operate in private or secret, He will be sure to provide a blessing upon us outwardly and publicly. This is wisdom for us. We must realize that sometimes not all those we label as friends are truly friends. Therefore, we must always be ready to guard our physical and spiritual being from those who may be like serpents, lurking for the right moment to attack us so we fall.

So, guard your dreams and your goals. No one needs to validate your message from God. If God has spoken a word to you then *Ken Yehi Ratzon*, meaning may it be His will!

God's spoken words are all that you need to claim victory in your life. "For as the rain and snow come down from heaven, and do not return there without watering the earth and making it produce and sprout, and providing seed to the sower and bread to the eater; So will My word be which goes out of My mouth; It will not return to Me empty, Without accomplishing what I desire, And without succeeding in the purpose for which I sent it." (*NASB*, Isa. 55.10-11).

WEEK 18 | ACTIVITY

The works that we do in private for God, will yield an outward blessing from Him. So, this week make a list of the things you would like to start doing to support the ministry of God. There's a long list of traditional items one can choose from, but the activity you decide to be a part of should be uniquely yours. Let's move past joining the activities that we think will get us the shout outs and public praises. What are the things you can start doing today that God will see and bless you for? Make that list then commit to start doing them this week.

_____

_____

_____

_____

_____

_____

_____

_____

_____

_____

_____

_____

19

"LET'S AVOID THAT CONVERSATION AT THE TABLE."

The Spiritual Message: Have a spirit of peace.

$\mathcal{I}$n your early school days, were you ever asked to choose an animal you wish you could be and given the opportunity to explain your choice to the class? Well, you may not be in elementary school anymore but here's an opportunity to ponder a question and choose between two options. Which animal, a dove or a serpent, best describes your spirituality?

Let's first look at Yeshua's words regarding doves and serpents. Yeshua (Jesus) said: "Pay attention! I am sending you out like sheep among wolves, so be as prudent as snakes and as harmless as doves" (*CJB*, Matt. 10.16). These words were from Yeshua's commission to his talmidim (disciples) to spread the message that the Kingdom of Heaven is near. In giving this instruction to his disciples Yeshua levied similes with a serpent and dove to amplify his message. Beyond this scripture though, doves and serpents are repeated in several biblical experiences which drive the metaphors that can be used for these animals.

Doves, particularly the ring-necked and diamond dove species, are the epitome of excellent family companions. These bird species are known for their soft cooing, innocuous nature, and social adeptness with humans. One can essentially say doves exemplify a peaceful spirit. In Genesis 8 we read of Noah and the dove. The dove was an obedient conduit that assisted Noah in identifying how much the water had receded after the flood. The dove carried out a mission that it was sent out to do – the mission was identifying life. This reminds me of the term *Sholiach* (Apostles) which means sent ones. These are brothers and sisters of faith that God has sent out on a mission to deliver a message, the message of His Kingdom. Doesn't this sound quite familiar to Yeshua's words in Matthew 10:16: " ...I am sending you out ... so be ... as <u>harmless</u> as doves." (*CJB*)? All believers are part of the mission of the gospel regardless of their role in a religious brick and mortar organization. We aren't part of the original 12 disciples, but Yeshua's work continues even to this day. Our role as a dove for Yeshua's work is being conduits or messengers of His teachings and doing that role with a peaceful spirit.

A peaceful spirit is important because without this our witnessing will fall flat with those we encounter. We can't be true *sent ones* or witnesses to unbelievers if we do not bear the right spirit. Our world is overflowing with hate, anger, rage, and malice. We live in a society where people carry disdain for their neighbor based on attributes like skin color. We as believers must be the antithesis of this; we must be the ones with a peaceful spirit. This may sound contrary to what the world tells us. But like doves, we must find calmness and solitude in knowing that God is in control and his words are sure and true. The promises that he has made for us, his children, will not return void. He will never leave us nor forsake us.

The serpent is on the opposite side of the coin. Some of the most dangerous animals in the world are of the snake species. The black mamba, for example, is the second largest venomous snake in the world with venom so potent that it can kill an adult human within minutes. When a black mamba attacks, instead of a single bit, it attacks repeatedly. As a result, the black mamba is known as one of the world's most aggressive animals. This dark and dangerous imagery of snakes is evident in the scriptures. In the bible, the serpent is associated with Satan. The Hebrew word for serpent used in the bible is *Nachash (נחש)*. This word is related to *Nechashim (נחשים)* which means chains. Who have we associated with chains and bondage? See Revelation chapter 20:1-2: "Then I saw an angel coming down from heaven. He had in his hand a key to the hole without a bottom. He also had a <u>strong chain</u>. He took hold of the dragon, that old snake, who is the Devil, or Satan, and <u>chained</u> him for 1,000 years" (*NLV*). The serpent is analogous to chains! But there is more. The serpent is also the symbol for sin, hypocrisy, and ultimately death. Yeshua labelled his challengers as brood of vipers (*NIV,* Matt 12.34) which we know are venomous snake species.

In essence, all things that are contrary to God and his instructions for us can be metaphorically described as attributes of the serpent. The text in Revelation 12:7-9 tells us: "And there was war in heaven, Michael and his angels waging war with the dragon. The dragon and his angels waged war, and they did not prevail, and there was no longer a place found for them in heaven. And the great dragon was thrown down, the serpent of old who is called the devil and Satan, who deceives the whole world; he was thrown down to the earth, and his angels were thrown down with him" (*NASB*).

It's quite lucid that those in our world that present behaviors that are of hate, anger, rage, and malice carry the spirit of the serpent and are consequentially of the camp of Satan. This is contrary to the peaceful spirit of a dove. So, to the original question, which animal is your walk with God symbolic of? Is it the serpent or the dove? Certainly, our lives should align with the dove, a symbol of righteousness, a symbol of peace. Though at times you may encounter individuals who create a challenge for you, remember to maintain your peace – a spiritual peace by taking refuge in God. Your peaceful approach to a contentious situation may just be the catalyst to bring that other person to a path of repentance.

WEEK 19 | ACTIVITY

What attributes do you have now that draws you back from being more dove-like in spirit? The only way we can improve our walk with God is by being honest with ourselves. He already sees and knows our hearts; we now must be honest with ourselves about the things we need to change to be more like Yeshua. This week, make a list of those behaviors that are detractors in your path to have a dove like spirit. After making your list I encourage you to pray to God using the words listed in Psalms 51:12: "Create in me a clean heart, God; renew in me a resolute spirit (CJB, Ps. 51.10)." Now make a conscious effort to avoid doing the things you listed which stops you from being the dove Yeshua wants you to be.

_____

_____

_____

_____

_____

_____

_____

_____

_____

_____

WEEK

"I THINK THE WAITER GOT HIM ANGRY."

The Spiritual Message: Avoid anger that leads to sin.

 *Y*ou may remember the 2003 comedy film titled Anger Management that starred Adam Sandler and Jack Nicholson. In this film Adam Sandler plays the role of a young businessman that loses his temper with a fellow- passenger on a plane. His loss of temper leads to a series of confrontational events on the plane with the flight attendant and sky marshal. Adam with his bull aggression causes the sky marshal to tase him. Adam then gets rewarded with the unorthodox sentence of anger management therapy with Dr. Buddy played by Jack Nicholson. A series of anger driven events spirals through the whole film where Adam goes as far as hurting his co-workers and wrecking the office when things does not pan out his way. This film is the perfect depiction of out-of-control anger.

I am sure you can relate to anger in some way. Maybe you know someone or have encountered someone that always seems to be angry and easily triggered with *last straw* moments. Or, if trivial life situations send you to the red zone instantaneously, maybe you become the angry person. Personally, I have been on the journey of dealing with my own anger. My issues could be traced to some undesirable family events in my early life. But after years of being irresponsible and failing to deal with the issues head-on, I realized

I wouldn't be a good husband, father, son, sibling, or leader in my community if I didn't fix it.

In the past, being on the last straw meant that I would quickly go to anger mode. Now, the last straw means it's time for me to turn to the best solution, God.

In James 1:19-20 the scripture tells us "You know this, my beloved brothers and sisters. Now everyone must be quick to hear, slow to speak, and slow to anger; for a man's anger does not bring about the righteousness of God" (*NASB*). James' words are an admonishment to believers against being quick to getting angry. Anger is an emotion that sprouts action. These actions can be detrimental to the person that's displaying anger, and detrimental to those interacting with the person. The emotion of anger can lead to actions of physical violence, and even hurtful and hateful speech. When these actions are perpetrated against others you have ventured into the world of unrighteousness.

Hurting another individual, be it physically or emotionally, is not exemplary of what we read in 1 John 4, a manual on love. "If someone says, *I love God*, and yet he hates his brother or sister, he is a liar; for the one who does not love his brother and sister whom he has seen, cannot love God, whom he has not seen. And this commandment we have from Him, that the one who loves God must also love his brother and sister" (*NASB*, 1 John 4.20-21). Loving one another is part of the instructions God has asked us to follow. And we know that following His instructions is righteousness (*NASB*, Deut. 6.25). The connection James was making to the believing community is that sprinting to anger will trigger actions that lead to unrighteousness. Walking the path that He designed for His Followers doesn't include indulging in the spirit of anger. Anger is truly obverse of God's wisdom: "One who is slow to anger has great understanding; But one who is quick-tempered exalts foolishness" (*NASB*, Prov. 14.29).

The bible is the greatest life manual you will ever encounter, its passages on anger became the guide that aided me to address my emotions so that I could be the person He needed me to be for others and ultimately to be a *shammash* or servant in His kingdom.

Now, am I saying that it's sinful to get angry? Not at all. We have examples of the most honorable fathers of our faith being angry for things of God. We remember Moses' anger burning towards the children of Israel for building the golden calf. And even Yeshua, our perfect example, driving the money traders out from the temple. Was Moses and Yeshua unrighteous for their anger? Absolutely not, Ephesians 4:26 reminds us to "be angry, and yet do not sin; do not let the sun go down on your anger" (*NASB*). God who created us in His perfect image enabled our beings with the emotion of anger. I believe God wants us to care so much for the things of His kingdom that it ignites an emotion of anger when the world operates outside of His instructions.

In those moments when our family, friends or acquaintances perpetrate evil, we should get angry at those things. Anger in those situations will inspire an action which would, hopefully, inspire change.

Be slow to getting angry for the trivial things in this world. Do not let your anger lead to unrighteousness like contempt, violence, and hatred. But recognize that we have the emotion of anger as a tool to inspire bold action for the things of God. It is not as complex as you think, God has provided us his inspired scriptures and examples of faithful fathers in our faith to use as an example on how we should live and deal with anger. Shalom.

WEEK 20 | ACTIVITY

What gets you angry to the point the subsequent actions are things you are later displeased about? Today I want you to make a list of the recent major blow ups you have had. Think about what caused those anger outbursts. Then after doing that, think about and write down what you could do differently next time to maintain your shalom, to maintain your peace. Apply the solutions you just noted whenever you find yourself in another situation that's driving you into the red zone. Be sure to note how the solutions you applied impacted the outcome of the situation, and how you felt about your actions. Additionally, whenever you find the spirit of anger presenting itself repeat these words:

Psalms 37:8, "Cease from anger and abandon wrath; Do not get upset; it leads only to evildoing" (*NASB*).

21

"SOMEONE JUST PAID YOUR BILL!"

The Spiritual Message: Your God is mighty!

A lion, the US Army, Super Man, Wonder Woman, Elohim – God. Considering their many attributes, what do these all have in common? One common theme is strength. I am sure brain images were generated as you read the list. You might have pictured a fierce lion being the ultimate predator, the king of the jungle. An image of advanced wartime machines and a large base of foot soldiers might have flooded your mental imagery for the US Army. Super man and Wonder Woman likely triggered animated or cinematic pictures of a man and woman with supernatural strength and abilities. But when you read '*Elohim-God*' what visuals sprung to your mind? Unlike a lion or the US Army, 7+ billion people across the world all experience God in a different way. Some people might have gotten visuals of a character they saw in a bible movie, some might have thought of the heavens, others might have thought of a face-less person sitting on a throne. There is a torrent of images one can have when 'God' is read. But one thing is certain, we all equate an uncapped power and strength to God. We call God the Mighty *El Gibbor*!

We see this translation of El Gibbor, the Mighty and Powerful God, referenced in our bibles. A clear image erupts of the warrior that God can be for us against our enemies. Psalms 24:8 reads: "Who is he, this glorious king? Adonai, strong and mighty, Adonai, mighty in battle" (*CJB*). This is the same God that provided the strength and ability for David to defeat Goliath. This would be the same God that delivered Israel from Egypt with a mighty hand and outstretched arm. Not only is God's might prevalent in battle, but God's might is prevalent through deliverance from non-combative troubles in our lives such as the sicknesses we face or the turbulent relationships we endure. God is powerful enough to provide His spirit to us so we can make it through arduous situations. God sent his son, directly of Him, to be our deliverer from all things. Isaiah 9:6 tells us this:

> For a Child will be born to us, a Son will be given to us; And the government will rest on His shoulders; And His name will be called Wonderful Counselor, Mighty God, Eternal Father, Prince of Peace (*NASB*).

In essence Yeshua will be all the things we need him to be in our struggles. He will be a father, a giver of wisdom, and a provider of spiritual peace to us.

It is great to know God has given us a gift that can be our deliverer from all things. However, I realize at times it can be difficult for some to grasp who God fully is. If you find yourself pondering on these things, my guidance to you is to turn to Isaiah 9:6 (*CJB*). Reading this passage can help you to learn or reaffirm who God is and has been to you through your life experiences, even though you have never seen God.

We believe God is real through tangible experiences in our lives, or through our faith and reading His word. But unlike a spouse or family member, we have never touched God. We cannot say we have seen the real God on television revealing himself through a weekly tele-broadcast or anything of that sort. We rely on our faith and life experiences to develop the story of who God is to us. I realize that can be hard, but that's what faith is. If you can believe, then that shows your trust in God. God desires followers who are willing to trust and put faith in Him.

I believe God is all powerful! I have endured strong hurricanes and frightening storms, and through those experiences I heard the deafening thunders that seemed to fall outside the measure of decibels. I have seen the bright lightings that looked like a knife seamlessly cutting through the air. I have seen and heard the torrential down pour of rain that made me think for a minute that I would be in the history books as a casualty of a major flood. These experiences of fear from the power and might of nature made me realize that if these earthly things are a product of God's design, how much greater is the designer? Furthermore, if the designer is Avi – my father, then that means I should never fear any enemy, situation, or dire circumstance because God is El Gibbor – mighty and powerful! He who is all powerful has control, so as His child I should not fear. Whatever you are going through, be it a need to transition to a new job, or new opportunities, deliverance from cancer or other severe sickness, know that your father is El Gibbor; He will stand in the gap for you and fight your fight ensuring that you will be delivered from your troubles.

WEEK 21 | ACTIVITY

You haven't seen God but recognize that He is El Gibbor fighting for you, consistently intervening on your behalf. This week's exercise is simple. This is your time to bask in the greatness of God and accept that He works for you. Test Him and see how He comes through for you! What are the top 12 things you would like to see Adonai resolve in your life? And we are not talking about the small things like a minor stomachache. Be specific. List those things you might think are impossible. This is God's specialty. He loves turning the seemingly impossible for man into the possible!

_____

_____

_____

_____

_____

_____

_____

_____

_____

_____

_____

_____

22

"THIS MEAL IS JUST PERFECT!"

The Spiritual Message: Be perfect like He is perfect.

What is perfection? For a while, I have pondered the state of perfection. Of the many words in the English lexicon, perfection seems to be one that stands out with great ambiguity. Perfection can be so subjective; one's state of perfection can differ from another person. The Webster's dictionary defines perfection as freedom from fault or defect, or an unsurpassable degree of accuracy or excellence. That definition seems logical when dealing with black and white topics like math. For example, if 1+X=2, then we know X must be equal to 1. The mathematical answer is clear cut, and the answer is universal. Now, if you got a series of those mathematical questions right it would be considered perfection. Anything less would be deemed imperfect.

How do you label perfection for the non-mathematical aspects of life, like being a great parent, mentor, or friend? Is there a right or wrong answer to define the bar of perfection? Take parenting for example. There's no universal way to parent perfectly. An action I may take as a parent may be regarded as a flaw to someone else when in fact it wasn't a flaw to me.

Since there's no singular standard for perfection, what do we really mean when we say we are seeking perfection? I believe in the minds of most people, seeking perfection is synonymous with being the best they can be. I believe it is for that reason the Webster's dictionary gives one definition of perfection as *an unsurpassable degree of accuracy or excellence.* I will add to that definition, perfection is *an attainment of a standard of excellence that one seeks to attain based on a personal or societal standard.*

Spending time with, learning to listen more, or setting great examples for my daughter might be what I base my standards for parenting excellence. But, while it is worthy to seek perfection in the familial areas in my life, it is most important to pursue perfection in a relationship with God. A perfect relationship with God yields the right benefits and outcomes for the other parts of our lives. However, that begs the question, "can you have a perfect relationship with God?" Salvador Dali says, "have no fear of perfection, you will never attain it". Are his words true? Is a perfect relationship with God impossible?

In Matthew 5:48 the text reads: "Therefore, be perfect, just as your Father in heaven is perfect" (*CJB*). Yeshua (Jesus) seemed to be clearly asking for a life of excellence from believers. But we read Rav Sha'ul (Paul) words in Romans 3:23: "for all have sinned and fall short of the glory of God" (*NASB*). It doesn't seem like Sha'ul was placing perfection as a possibility, right? Let's return to Yeshua's words in Matthew 5:48. Prior to Yeshua speaking on perfection He made a list of admonishments found in Matthew 5:43-48:

> You have heard that our fathers were told, 'Love your neighbor — and hate your enemy.' But I tell you, love your enemies! Pray for those who persecute you! Then you will become children of your Father in heaven. For he makes his sunshine on good and bad people alike, and he sends rain to the righteous and the unrighteous alike. What reward do you get if you love only those who love you? Why, even tax-collectors do that! And if you are friendly only to your friends, are you doing anything out of the ordinary? Even the

> Goyim (Gentiles) do that! Therefore, be perfect, just
> as your Father in heaven is perfect (*CJB*).

In short, Matthew 5:48 means that if you love all people, regardless of their feelings towards you, then you would be walking, or being just like God! Our life's purpose is to be *perfect* imitators of God. Being perfect therefore doesn't mean to be flawless, but it refers to being in a state of maturity or completeness. The Greek word used in the text is *teleios,* it means completeness, or maturity.

In my journey towards being what God wants me to be, I'm expected to stumble and make mistakes. Which is why God provided guides to teach us how to repent to Him and to each other. Being in a state of perfection before God means that you will be mature enough to repent when you wrong a brother or sister. This seems like a contradiction to western ideology. However, if you isolate your mind from the western paradigm, you will understand how this makes sense. For example, when a baby is born you may look at that child, kiss him or her, and say words like she/he is just perfect! The essence of the word 'perfect', in this example, focuses on the child's birth and presence. It's not isolated to the importance that the beholder places on subjective attributes such as the child's skin tone, eye color, or hair type.

We can attain a state of perfection in our walk with God. If this was not true Yeshua would not have mentioned those words to us. To the wealthy man Yeshua said, "If you want to be perfect, go, sell your possessions and give to the poor, and you will have treasure in heaven. Then come, follow me" (*NIV*, Matt. 19.21). We know this story well, the wealthy man left and did not follow Yeshua because his heart was not in a complete state to seek after God, his immature heart was on his riches.

What's the point to all of this? The point is this, you can attain perfection in your walk with God, because perfection in your walk with God is simply just you willingly doing what He has asked of you. What has God asked us to do? Love others, make peace, and walk in His commandments and ways. You can be complete like He is complete. And better yet, He wants completeness for you.

WEEK 22 | ACTIVITY

Hopefully, your eyes have been opened to a different way of thinking about perfection. With this view of perfection, how can you grow in your walk with Yeshua? What are the things that are preventing you from getting to your complete state in God? Is it a boyfriend, a job, a habit that you have been facing for years? Whatever it is, you can overcome it and get to the pristine relationship you desire to have with God. There are both spiritual and physical blessings in store by getting to that place. Today, make the decision that the things that are constricting you from moving closer to God will no longer be detractors in your life. Draw two circles, in one circle list the detractors negatively impacting your relationship with God, in the second circle list the promoters positively impacting your relationship with God. Draw a line through every detractor. These are the behaviors you will commit to cease doing. Then highlight every promoter. Every day for the next two weeks, focus on implementing more promoters into your daily life. Then pause on the journey and take stock of your intimacy with God. Acknowledge your increased maturity in your walk with God toward your path to spiritual perfection.

The hope is that as you focus more on the positive promoters, you will be driven to carry out these behaviors over and over, and ultimately develop a more complete relationship with Adonai.

_____

_____

_____

_____

_____

_____

23
WEEK

"I HATE THIS MEAL!"

The Spiritual Message: God's way is loving love and hating hate.

While many in our society might be in denial, hate is a very real problem today. It's real in all of the 50 states, 5 major territories, and various minor islands that comprise the United States of America. According to the FBI's Uniform Crime Reporting (UCR) Program, in 2019 there were over 7,000 incidents of hate crimes across the United States. The reasons for hate crimes are diverse; they can be motivated by religious views, race, sexual orientation, gender and even someone's physical or emotional disability. One grievous hate crime that occurred in 2019, is the mass shooting in El Paso, Texas at a Walmart that left 22 people dead and another 23 people severely injured. The shooter purposefully targeted Hispanic individuals at the Walmart. On the day of the shooting the perpetrator uploaded a document to the internet that stated: "This attack is a response to the Hispanic invasion of Texas. They are the instigators, not me. I am simply defending my country from cultural and ethnic replacement brought on by the invasion." This perpetrator showed evidence of a willful contemplation to harm the lives of those that looked different than he did.

As I reflect on past hate crimes, I try to comprehend why people develop the feelings they do toward another person. Feelings that could ultimately lead to heinous acts. For examples, I think back to

Hitler and his plot to destroy the Jews resulting in the murders of 6 million of God's people or the ~17 million Africans that died through the harsh transatlantic slave trade by the hands of European traders. Why do people, who are all created in the image of God, believe they have a superior status than their fellow brother or sister? It is truly mind boggling that people can develop the tenacity to do evil acts under the notion of superiority.

Leviticus 19:17 tells us clearly: "Do not hate your brother in your heart ..." *(CJB)*. Hate is the antithesis of love, it's the highest level of unrighteousness that Satan uses to control mankind. Satan was removed from the heavenlies because he wanted to be God. His pride clouded his purpose, consequently he is now the adversary that represents everything God stands against.

Understand that Satan realizes hate is the most stealth tool he has in his arsenal to keep us away from God. Why is this? Well humans were created with emotion. We cry, laugh, and get angry at times based on our experiences. We then leverage those experiences to craft our behavior for future situations. The thing is, because emotions are such a natural part of us, we can develop feelings that are in line with hate. These feelings fester when gone unchecked, blossoming into radical ideologies and behaviors that yield evil acts against others.

You might believe Satan operates through apparent temptation like leaving $10K in bank rolls on your office desk that you know is not yours. But the temptations from Satan are more covert than that. It's the situations where you drive on the highway, someone cuts you off then you take that opportunity to place a degrading or negative label on that person and their entire race. Or taking the opportunity to feed into theories and chatter from friends and family that labels a person because of their facial features or attire. These are the covert opportunities Satan uses to stir up hate in our hearts so that we can be the apotheosis of what God dislikes. Satan knows if he can set the spirit of hate in us, he will be successful at separating us from the love of God.

Unlike Satan, God is love. He admonishes us all to love. He told us to love him, and then to love our neighbors as ourselves. Yeshua's words are, on the premise of those two mitzvahs (commandments) all the Torah and the Prophets are dependent (*CJB,* Matt. 22.40). If we truly love God then we cannot hate the people that we see every day – we cannot love who we have not seen while hate who we do see (*CJB,* 1 John 4.20).

We must also be careful that we are not mislabeling our hate as dislike based on a laundry list of shallow reasons. I think, when given the opportunity, we sometimes rationalize our hate and mollify it by calling that hate "dislike." God certainly knows our heart, there is nothing we can hide or mask from him. To ensure we can always present ourselves as holy and acceptable before Him, we should be mindful of the feelings we label as dislike. Watch out for this behavior. In the words of my Spanish professor from college "Tengo Cuidado!"

In short, we must show love to each other regardless of religious views, race, sexual orientation, gender and even someone's physical or emotional disability. We are all created in His image, therefore rather than finding a reason to hate, we should always find an excuse to love each other. It is through love we can turn hearts to God. This is how Adonai has called us to live, loving love and hating hate.

WEEK 23 | ACTIVITY

It's so easy for us to have feelings fester in our hearts. Before we know it, we have developed a heart of stone for people that we should be loving and sharing God's word with. Take 15 minutes today to do a self-examination. Is there someone or a group of people you have developed ill feelings towards? When did this feeling start? How did this feeling come to be? By answering these questions, you will begin to get to the core of the feelings that could be the source of hate you have for someone or a group of people. After you have done this personal examination, walk the new path of accepting love in your heart for this person or group of people. Remember God created us all. We are all from Him, created in His image. We can't have hate for others yet claim we love Adonai. May this day be a start to a new journey free of hate from your heart. Besides, as one person puts it, it takes too much work to hate, to love is like an unending vacation.

_____

_____

_____

_____

_____

_____

_____

_____

_____

24
WEEK

"LET ME RECOMMEND THE BEST APPETIZER."

The Spiritual Message: Only consider wise counsel.

When I was in elementary school our teacher would randomly select students to supervise the class when she needed to go to a faculty meeting or needed to be absent for some non-academic reason. The appointed student would ensure everyone completed their assignments and would strive to keep order in the classroom. It was an early lesson of responsibility and bearing leadership. As you can imagine that student-in-chief had lots of attention. Kids who never spoke to you before wanted to speak to you. The kids that always wanted to fight you now sought to be your friends. Everyone tried to be nice to the student-in-chief, no one wanted to be on the punishment list. Well, during this euphoria of stardom, there were a faction of kids that would volunteer themselves to be the self-appointed consiglieres – the advisors to the student-in-chief. These kids self-appointed themselves as advisors, giving unsolicited counseling on who should dispose the trash, who had been naughty, who should be written up, or who should be given lines to write as immediate punishment. It was quite the thing to see back in my elementary school. But the reason I share this experience is to highlight the observation I had then. My observation was everyone wanted to feel valuable by being the advisor to the person in charge.

The observation I had then with my classmates, is true for adults today. Have you ever found yourself in a position where you felt stuck in trying to make a good decision, but you hear conflicting reasoning from the people who are giving you advice? That can certainly be a tough situation to be in, especially when making decisions on careers and relationships.

Proverbs 1:5 tells us: "A wise person will hear and increase in learning, and a person of understanding will acquire wise counsel" (*NASB*). That text from the scriptures makes us understand that prudent folks should seek after wise counsel. But what is wise counsel? That text in Proverbs 1:5 doesn't tell us what is considered wise or unwise. But examining Psalms 1:1 can offer additional insight. The text says: "Blessed is the person who does not walk in the counsel of the wicked ..." That translation is from the NASB, but I like the CJB's translation: "How blessed are those who reject the advice of the wicked ..."

What makes a certain counsel or advice wise is the basis on which it is asserted. Is the advice based on biblical principles or on the principles of the world? Is the advice contrary to the commands of Adonai? Wisdom is the perfect execution of knowledge – and in this case the execution of knowledge that is sourced from God.

God has given us knowledge by way of his commands, Yeshua's teachings, and the teachings of the prophets – it is through these we can have the soundest knowledge. So, for clarity, if the advice you are receiving is contrary to the word of God, then the advice you received is not to be considered wise counsel, it is bad advice, it is bad counsel.

1 Kings 12 puts unwise counsel in full display. Here we have King Rehoboam being addressed by the assembly of Israel, they begged for King Rehoboam to turn a new chapter and ease the burden his father King Solomon placed on them. King Rehoboam did the right thing of seeking counsel. He went to the elders for counsel, and they encouraged him to be a true servant leader and speak kindly to Israel. King Rehoboam took an additional step though, he went on to seek counsel from the younger men that grew up with him. Those men gave the king advice contrary to the elders; the young men advised the king to speak harshly to Israel telling Israel he will discipline

them with scorpions! The advice from the youth was unwise. It was unwise because God's instruction on shunning pride, honing humility, and loving your neighbor as yourself were all undermined from the advice of putting great hardship on the Israelites. If you read on in 1 Kings 12 you then see that this unwise advice drove the contentious split of Israel into two kingdoms.

Having great counsel in life is a necessity. We all need the wisdom of others who have gone through similar experiences or have insight based on their general experiences. But to ensure we never go astray and make avoidable detrimental life choices; we should always seek out wise advice. As we have learned, wise advice is that which is based on the morals and principles of God's word. If you are in a place today where you feel stuck, and you question if you have been given wise advice, you should test the words shared with you against the things in His word. If it doesn't hold up it's time to acquire wise counsel.

WEEK 24 | ACTIVITY

If you are at a crossroads and need to make a critical decision in your life, consider counsel that is wise. We know wise counsel is one that is based on God's words. To aid you with the crossroads you are facing, seek out a believer that you know stands honestly on God's word. I encourage you to get advice from this person. Discuss the matter with them and pray with that person. Have that person be your prayer partner as you embark on your decision making. The body of Messiah exists so we can support and serve each other. And on the flipside, you should also be a person that can be a similar pillar of support for wise counsel to others that are in need.

_____

_____

_____

_____

_____

_____

_____

_____

_____

_____

_____

25

WEEK

"IT TASTES SO GOOD, TRUST MY WORDS."

The Spiritual Message: Listen to God's messengers.

There was a father who ran a small-time construction company for over 40 years. This humble father had a son that he made great sacrifices for to ensure the son would attain great success in his lifetime. The son went on to a technical college and learned about more advanced techniques in construction. The father was proud of his son's educational accomplishments. When the son returned home after completing his college studies, he worked in his father's company putting into action all that he had learned. Soon the son began to feel like he was invaluable to the company. One day, his father said, "son I want you to take the lead on your first project." The father asked the son to oversee this one-day project to complete the paving of a residential driveway. The one admonishment the father gave to his son was to only use three tradesmen that have been with the father for over 40 years.

The son got on the project and was eager to show his knowledge and how better and more skilled he was than his father. He used his fanciest of tools and technology on this project; he was eager to finish the job quicker than the typical time just so he could show how much of a construction savant he was. He realized he needed one other body to finish the project quicker. He ran some math and figured if he got a laborer and allowed them to work for just a few hours he could still be under budget and his father would be impressed with him.

One hour before the job would typically be finished, the father showed up with a group of leaders from the largest construction company in the area. You see, this was his father's chance to get a lead role in one of the biggest projects in the city. The men were in the middle of negotiations to get the father and his men on the big city project. They were going to give the father the chance to lead the pavement portion of the project, but all they wanted to do was see some of his guys in action on a paving project before finalizing the deal. When they showed up the son had already completed the job. The father ran to his son and said why is everyone sitting around? The son responded, are you impressed? I finished this work a lot sooner than you expected. The father touched his son by the face and said, maybe in any other situation I would have been impressed, but today more than ever I needed you to listen.

Learning to be still and to listen to the instructions of others can be hard for some. We always feel as though our intelligence sets us apart. As a result, we think we should always be independent without taking heed or instructions from others. The scriptures have taught us it is quite unwise to always rely on your own knowledge and abandon listening to others.

Proverbs 1:5 says:

> Someone who is already wise will hear and learn still more; someone who already understands will gain the ability to counsel well (*CJB*).

In James 1:19, James admonishes:

> Therefore, my dear brothers, let every person be quick to listen but slow to speak, slow to get angry (*CJB*).

Shema is the Hebrew word for listen or hear in the bible. This is the same word Elohim (God) used when He took the children of Israel out of Egypt and prepared them to enter the promised land. His words to them in Deuteronomy 6:4 was "*Shema Yisrael*," or Hear Yisrael (*CJB*). This was a special call out to Israel to listen to His instructions so that they could be preserved in this new and bountiful land they were about to enter.

God sends family, friends, and even those we have branded as enemies to be his messengers to us. If we choose not to listen to the messengers He has sent us, how can we overcome the obstacles we are facing in our lives so we can experience the bountiful blessings He has in store for us? We kneel and pray asking Elohim for deliverance but, in many cases, he has sent the deliverance. He has sent crisp instructions on what he needs us to do. Instead of listening to His instructions we have turned a deaf ear to his words and have decided to do our own will.

I have heard people say in the past "I listen only to God, no one can say anything to me." Albeit harsh, this in direct terms is a diabolical statement. Not listening to the people God has sent His messages through, is plainly not listening to God. This is analogical to hating people you see yet claiming to love God who you have not seen. The message you receive may not always be what you were expecting to hear, but God's words do not return void. He understands it all, we must have complete trust in Him, we must trust His message to us – His message is right for us. We must learn to listen to Him, and by extension that means accepting those He has sent His messages through. Failing to listen will only yields heartaches and problems.

WEEK 25 | ACTIVITY

If you have been shunning God, either directly or through His messengers, now is the time to take a pause and recalibrate. We may have our own ideas of how we would like the direction of our life to be or our own thinking of how God should answer our prayers. Newsflash, the human mind is beyond inferior to the mind of God. Therefore, stop relying on yourself and trust the direction that comes from God. Take an inventory of the items you have been waiting for God to give direct guidance on. Now, reflect on advice, messages, or situations that have occurred over recent months. Do you think a direction was given that you closed your eyes to? Was an answer given that you covered your ears to? Pray this prayer as you go through this week and reflect on whether you have missed His signs:

> *Abba Father, I know you are abundant in knowledge, please show mercy to me. Please open my ears, and heart to receive your message. I want to be your sheep that truly knows your voice. I want to discern your words so that I stay on your path always; I want to live the life that you have ordained for me.*
>
> *Amein.*

_____

_____

_____

_____

_____

26

"OOPS, I MADE A MESS."

The Spiritual Message: Forgiveness is golden.

Loving the deserving is easy. But loving or showing great kindness to the undeserving is a challenge to many. It can be hard extending love to the seemingly undeserving folks that show you hate. When dealing with the folks that mistreat us, we struggle with the 'F' word – Forgiveness. Many of us find it hard to forgive those that have wronged us, it's a mental and emotional battle that we face-off against. Sometimes we lose that battle because we resort to not forgiving. Quite frankly it usually feels better to not forgive. It's easier to let your natural emotions run its course of being mad or repeating the wronged scenario over and over in your mind, creating a repetitive mental loop in your brain. Is this the way we should live as children of the Most High? Certainly not.

In Luke 15:11-32 we read of what has been branded the story of the prodigal son. We recount that a father had two sons, and one of the sons asked for his inheritance so that he could depart from his father. After this son received his inheritance, he left his father's place for a far country. Upon getting to this new land, away from his father, the son engaged in reckless living. After a short-time, he squandered the inheritance he received. With no inheritance left, coupled with a famine in the land, the son opted to return home to his father.

The scriptures tell us that while his son was a long way off his father saw him then ran towards him. His son greeted him with a repentant spirit and was willing to be accepted as less than an heir. However, the words of the father found in Luke 15: 22-24 are: "Quickly bring out the best robe and put it on him, and put a ring on his finger and sandals on his feet; and bring the fattened calf, slaughter it, and let's eat and celebrate; for this son of mine was dead and has come to life again; he was lost, but now he has been found!' And they began celebrating" (*NASB*).

In essence, the father theatrically welcomed his son home with wide-open arms, forgiving the past thinking no less of his son. The father openly forgave. Of course, this recount is the epitome of God's relationship with us his creation. If we run back to Elohim with repentance, He will forgive us and accept us again as one of His children. However, what we cannot miss from the text is that this comparison of God's willingness to forgive us does not stop at the celestial level. The level of forgiveness shown by the father to his once lost son is also a lesson for how believers should forgive.

In Matthew 6:12, a passage that most people know very well, Yeshua taught us how to pray to the Father. In praying to the Father, Yeshua told us to say: "And forgive us our debts, as we also have forgiven our debtors" (*NASB).* In other words, Yeshua is inferring that if we are asking God to forgive us, then we are acknowledging that we too have forgiven those that have wronged us. Are we forgiving others to the same degree we are running to Adonai for forgiveness? Are we forgiving without limits, or do we hold a scorecard of the wrongs carried out against us?

In Matt 18:21-22, we read of the encounter with Peter and Yeshua on the topic of forgiveness. In verse 21 Peter asked Yeshua what's the optimal number of times one should forgive. Peter notes seven times as an optimal number. Why seven in the first place? A usual explanation is that the Rabbis of that time thought three was the optimal number of times to forgive someone. Consequently, the interpretation is that Peter was being generous in his selection of seven. I differ a bit on that thinking. My perspective is if Peter was trying to be magnanimous, wouldn't saying six (indicative of doubling the Rabbis' number) or four (1 more than the Rabbis' recommendation) be more practical? I think there is more happening than Peter just being artificially generous. I believe Peter had a biblical base to his reasoning.

Proverbs 24:16 says a righteous man falls seven times (*CJB*). After being forgiven seven times – the number associated with perfection - you are now at "perfection" or better translated an expectation of "fullness", or "maturity." Therefore, after falling seven times there's no expectation you would continue to mess up like you did before. It's not a skewed spiritual thinking. But Yeshua had to provide Peter a grander picture and meaning.

In Matt 18:22, Yeshua responds to Peter by stating "No, not seven times, but seventy times seven!" (*CJB*). What does Yeshua's response mean? Here is an abbreviated breakdown. Yeshua said to forgive 70x7, when you examine the product of 70 and 7 the result is 490. This number is important, not important to note as a cap or limitation on forgiveness, but quite the opposite. The gematria, or alphanumeric code in Hebrew, for the number 490 is תמים/Tamim. Tamim means to be complete, perfect, or blameless. This is the same word used in Proverbs 28:18: "Whoever lives <u>blamelessly</u> will be saved, but he whose ways are crooked will fall in one [of those ways]" (*CJB*).

This word Tamim is seen again in Deuteronomy 18:13: "You are to be <u>blameless</u> before the LORD your God" (*NASB*). What is Yeshua saying? Yeshua was telling Peter to be blameless before God; you cannot cap the number of times you forgive! Forgive to the same measure Adonai forgives you for your sins – which is limitless. Otherwise, if you cap your forgiveness then you are not standing without blame when you stand before God seeking forgiveness for your own sins.

This, my friends, is the reason why we need to forgive. Forgiveness is greater than the person who wronged you, forgiveness is the key ingredient to the relationship that the Father desires to have with you – one that's untethered or unbroken by the imperfection that comes with unforgiveness.

WEEK 26 | ACTIVITY

Consider this week's activity to be life changing. Who do you hold a grudge in your heart for at this moment? If there's anyone that you have been holding back forgiveness from, now is the time to change that. Consider this, what if God chose to not forgive you? List the name and contact for each person you know you need to forgive. Over the course of the next week, I want you to pray and ask for the spirit and courage to reach out to all these individuals. Reach out and give to them the forgiveness God has given to you.

_____

_____

_____

_____

_____

_____

_____

_____

_____

_____

_____

27

"IT'S PROBABLY BEST I DON'T EAT ANYMORE"

The Spiritual Message: God wants us to take care of ourselves.

If you spend enough time on social media, you will likely encounter a few posts where someone is highlighting their need for self-care, or they are broadcasting how they are engaging in their much-deserved self-care time. Self-care time to the world can entail enjoying the priciest massage sessions the city has to offer, or even jetting off to the most luxurious vacation spots across the world. For some, this may provide an immediate relief from the stresses that the world bears on us. But most times these pleasures can prove to be ephemeral; at some point you return to the usual chaos of life after that fun trip, or you return home from that expensive massage session to still lay in bed tormented to the point of insomnia. True self-care does not have to be planned around the accumulation of vacation hours, or by the size of your paycheck. The best self-care is one that aligns to taking care of the temple – your body – in the exact way God intended.

In 1 Corinthians 3:16-17, Sha'ul (Paul) says: "Don't you know that you people are God's temple and that God's Spirit lives in you? So, if anyone destroys God's temple, God will destroy him. For God's temple is holy, and you yourselves are that temple" (*CJB*).

Paul's word in this passage targeted the community of believers that were creating discord amongst themselves, which was destroying the body of believers. But most importantly, from Paul's words we gained a valuable nugget about the value of our earthly bodies. We understand from Paul's comments that God's Ruach (Spirit, Breath) lives in us, therefore we can never approach our earthly bodies as a mere vessel worth abusing. Since God's Spirit dwells in us we should refrain from doing all the things that would shun His Spirit. This includes tearing down each other (1 Cor 3:3), sexual immorality, and lasciviousness (Gal 5:19-21).

In understanding the value of our earthly bodies, a conduit for Adonai's Spirit, how can we ensure we take care of our body – His temple – to ensure we are in a state to be the best conduit for the work of God? What is the real spiritual based self-care we should be applying to our lives daily? I believe there are six basic principles that will ensure that we all as believers can have the body that is able to be used by God for his work.

The six self-care actions that believers should effectuate are: taking the right rest, eating according to His way, abstaining from sexual immorality, abstaining from drunkenness, halting anxiety, and engaging in physical activity. I know what your thoughts are right now, there's no way all this is spelled out in the bible. Let's explore this.

Taking The Right Rest

In Exodus 20 God gave the ten commandments, or ten mitzvot. These are the commandments that all those who seek to be His followers should do to show their love for Him (John 14:15). The fourth commandment given in Exodus 20:8-10 is: "Remember the Sabbath Day, to keep it holy. For six days you shall labor and do all your work, but the seventh day is a Sabbath of the Lord your God ..." (*NASB*).

God rested on the seventh day after He completed his work of creation. If our all mighty and unmatchable Abba can find the time to rest from the work of His hands, we who were created in His image should be no different. Resting on the days that God has ordained in His word keeps us from the typical burnout that overtakes our society.

We may not always understand the reason for God's instructions, but we can certainly trust that his instructions are perfect for us (*CJB*, Ps. 19.7). Leviticus 23 details the perfect holiday schedule that God wants for His children. This doesn't mean we shouldn't take other personal holidays. The point is, if we ensure to at least take the days listed in Leviticus 23 to be off from the bustles of the world, we will be giving the right care to our bodies, the care that God intended.

Eating According to His Way

According to the Center for Science in the Public Interest, every year about 678,000 deaths in the US are tied to bad diets. Additionally, the Lancet claims that 11 million deaths in the world are tied to poor diet. It is a fact, that every time humans deviate from the ways of God, we pay the ultimate price; we pay with our lives. The statistic on poor diet amplifies the point that our own views on what and how we should eat is a path that leads to death instead of a path that leads to life. God is the greatest dietician your money can't afford. In Leviticus 11 He gave us explicit guidance on the types of animals we can have culinary freedoms with it. He also gave us instructions against eating foods with blood (*CJB*, Lev. 17.10). All these were given as a guide to keeping our temples in a state ready to receive His Spirit. So, though self-care for the world may be enjoying exotic alligator meals with friends, the Creator has better intentions for His people that will yield true blessings that are not just ephemeral.

Abstaining From Sexual Immorality

In 1 Corinthians 6:13 we read: "Food is meant for the stomach and the stomach for food? Maybe, but God will put an end to both of them. Anyhow, the body is not meant for sexual immorality but for the Lord, and the Lord is for the body" (*CJB*). Paul highlights that sexual immorality is a grave sin against the body, unlike other sins. Therefore, as believers who seek after Adonai's presence, sexual immorality must be far from us (*CJB*, Eph. 5:3). True biblical self-care can never be complete if sexual immorality is found amongst us. (*For a list of some forbidden practices see Leviticus 18*).

Abstaining From Drunkenness

Ephesians 5:18 tells us: "And do not get drunk with wine, in which there is debauchery, but be filled with the Spirit!" (*NASB*). This infers that if we are drunk the Spirit cannot dwell in us. In other words, drunkenness becomes a part of the list of evils that destroys God's temple (*NASB,* 1 Cor. 3.17). Drunkenness impacts our mind, and this is important because mental awareness is what we need so that we can avoid being in a state where we are easily deceived by the adversary and fall into grave sins. Therefore, we must always seek to be in a sober place (*NASB,* 1 Pet. 5.8). Biblical self-care does not mean a rebuke against having wine, but the guidance is against going to a place of overindulgence that leads to drunkenness – this destroys the temple of Adonai, your body.

Halting Anxiety

Yeshua, our great Rabbi, told us in Matthew 6:25-26 that we should not worry. "Therefore, I tell you, don't worry about your life, what you will eat or drink; or about your body, what you will wear. Isn't life more than food and the body more than clothing? Look at the birds of the air flying about! They neither plant nor harvest, nor do they gather food into barns; yet your heavenly Father feeds them. Aren't you worth more than they?" (*CJB*). Research shows that stress is the major source of illness in 75% to 90% of diseases that astronomically impact our quality of life. To live a more full and complete life, Yeshua admonishes us to practice greater faith by leaning more on Him for all our needs. Cease worrying about all the uncertainties that exist in this world and focus more on God.

Engaging In Physical Activity

Some people might not equate biblical self-care to physical activity, but physical activity is needed. In 1 Timothy 4:8 Paul mentioned: "For although physical exercise does have some value, godliness is valuable for everything, since it holds promise both for the present life and the life to come." (*CJB*). I have heard some people use this verse to advocate against exercise, but a more careful review of the text proves otherwise. Notice Paul said, "physical exercise does have <u>some value</u>." 1 Timothy 4:8 said differently would go something like this: engaging in frequent exercising would prove futile if you are an unrighteous person living an ungodly life. So, the admonishment from Paul is that exercise is good, when it goes along with righteous living.

Physical activity is needed for our bodies to be at the optimum level of health so we can be in the best health to serve Adonai. It has been best said by one Rabbi, "if you intentionally do the things that make you unhealthy then that's sin; because when you become sick and cannot serve God to the fullest, and carry out his commandments due to your limitations, then you have in essence, intentionally done the things to break his commandments".

In summation, the best self-care is the one that aligns with taking care of our temple – our body – in a way that God's Spirit can dwell in us. Conducting this biblically minded self-care allows you to live out His purpose for you while on earth. Effectuating the six basic actions on biblical self-care, resting, eating properly, being sexually responsible, avoiding drunkenness, being stress-free, and staying fit, will yield the true connection we seek with our Abba Adonai – this will grant us blessings in this world and the next.

WEEK 27 | ACTIVITY

My hope is that the six basic biblical self-care principles become principles you can engage in immediately. Examine the six principles, are there items on the list of principles you know you need to pay special attention to in your life? Make a list of those principles you haven't been complying with, then next to each principle list the actions you can take, starting from this week, to comply with the principles. Remember, the six self-care principles are all based on God's word, so complying with the list will yield you direct benefits from our Creator.

_____

_____

_____

_____

_____

_____

_____

_____

_____

_____

_____

_____

_____

28

"I MISS DOING BRUNCH WITH DAD."

The Spiritual Message: God understands our grief.

*W*hen you are young and still naïve about the dangers of the world, the reality of death might not always connect with you. It doesn't connect because you think that death won't happen to you or your close family. At some point in your life it will happen, you will lose a close friend, a parent, or sibling. The reality of death is now in your personal atmosphere. In that moment you feel great anguish and grief as you are acclimating to the sense of loss you are newly experiencing.

Regardless of who you are, we all become susceptible to the effects of grief. These effects include suicidal thoughts, physiological distress, compulsive obsession of the past, anxiety and even the apprehension of the future. Grief can cripple the best of us. But there's hope. We shouldn't look at grief as that major exam that we have to conquer on our own, here is where we need to look to God, as He too understands grief.

On a stormy night back in 2010 lying in bed just waiting for the storm to pass I got a phone call. My cell phone luminated signaling "Dad." My first assumption when I saw the call was that it was just an innocent phone call. Perhaps he was doing a welfare call or probably needed my assistance in typing out a document. I answered the call, but it wasn't the voice of my father greeting me. Instead, someone was on the line notifying me that my father just suffered a heart attack, and he was unresponsive. The first words from my mouth were "he will be alright, right?" It was storming greatly, trees were down, poles obstructed the streets, and darkness filled our area because electricity went out. This ordeal from the storm made it arduous for medical assistance to timely help my ailing father. I still believed all would be alright, but then reality finally set in. The words came, "He has expired." The person who was a great source of my identity was no longer alive. This was the moment I truly experienced grief. It felt like someone cut my very soul and heart straight from my chest leaving me hollow. As a recent graduate from business school, I felt like my life was about to take off. The loss of my father changed it all for me. I asked questions I couldn't find the right answers to. The world felt dark and gloomy.

The good news is, while in the darkness, a light, obscured by grief but always present, began to get more apparent through the thickness of the dark clouds. That light was Yeshua.

It may appear cliché to some to just simply say Adonai was there for me in my moment of grief, but truly He was there. His presence became apparent through fellow believers, and even in the still moments when no one was around. Other believing brothers, sisters, mothers, and fathers in Yeshua reminded me of the words of Paul in 1 Thessalonians 4:13-17:

> Now, brothers, we want you to know the truth about those who have died; otherwise, you might become sad the way other people do who have nothing to hope for. For since we believe that Yeshua died and rose again, we also believe that in the same way God, through Yeshua, will take with him those who have died. When we say this, we base it on the Lord's own word: we who remain alive when the Lord comes will certainly not take precedence over those who have died. For the Lord himself will come down from heaven with a rousing cry, with a call from one of the

ruling angels, and with God's *shofar*; those who died united with the Messiah will be the first to rise; then we who are left still alive will be caught up with them in the clouds to meet the Lord in the air; and thus we will always be with the Lord (*CJB*).

The sadness we experience in this world can cause us to forget what really matters in the end. We must never forget that we are in this world for a moment, but after this we look forward to eternity with our true father.

Adonai our father understands pain and grief too, so who else better to run to for comfort? Adonai gave His son, His only begotten son, so that we can have a life with him after death. As a parent, can you imagine, giving your only child up to save the life of someone else? Good earthly parents will never make that decision to give up their only child to save the life of any other. This hard choice, that we as earthly parents would never make, is what God did for us all. Yeshua cried, "My God! My God! Why have you deserted me" (*CJB*, Matt. 27:46)? One can only imagine the pain of the Father as he heard these words. Nonetheless, He signed up for this grief because He loves humanity that much.

God understands the pain we bear when we too, His creation, experience our dire moments of grief. He promises to be a comforter to us all (*CJB*, Isa. 51.11-12), so we should feel confident in His promise for comfort. Let the tears fall as we are emotional beings, we feel, and we care, that is how God made us, but let's remember that death is another stop on this journey called life. Therefore, let's not mourn like those who have no hope, mourning through suicidal behavior and turning against God – essentially exemplifying the behavior that will separate us from His love. But let us instead draw closer to God who has borne the ultimate grief by giving His only Son for us all. Let's look forward to the eternal life that is before us.

WEEK 28 | ACTIVITY

If you are experiencing grief right now, I would like you to spend time reflecting on the words of Paul in 1 Thessalonians 4:13-17. In addition, my hope is that you can feel comfortable reaching out to your fellow brothers and sisters in the faith. When one person mourns, we all mourn and support each other.

If you are not mourning or suffering the effects of grief right now, maybe you know someone that is. If you do know someone that is mourning, be a pillar of support to that person, reach out and pray with that person, make the time to visit them and provide the support they need to get through their grief. Let's all be a fountain of strength to our family in Messiah.

_____

_____

_____

_____

_____

_____

_____

_____

_____

_____

29

WEEK

"DURING BRUNCH THEY SHOULD PLAY LESS VILE MUSIC."

The Spiritual Message: Guard your mind.

One afternoon while working remotely, I ventured downstairs to the living room for a short break from my hectic day, which was nowhere near complete. I reclined into the sofa and turned on the television to relieve my mind of numbers and spreadsheets. While watching, a commercial marketing a Burger King burger special aired. The interesting thing about the commercial wasn't the product itself, there wasn't anything enticing about the product that caught my attention. What caught my attention was the double entendre and subliminal sexual innuendo employed in the commercial. With the image of the King mascot apparent, and millennial aged folks eating into the burger, the voice over mentioned something to the effect of "grab hold of the King's buns, with both hands." Anyone reading this surely knows that buns are also euphemisms for what we call buttocks. I couldn't help but take the time to focus on the fact that there are millions of people that would see this commercial, and the message in the commercial would subconsciously shape some part of the viewers thoughts. Sadly, this style of commercial isn't unique. Thousands of commercials air all the time using similar or even more explicitly sexual and derogatory messages. Messages, embedded within advertisements, music, movies, and casual television shows, impact our minds and ultimately our actions. To stay grounded in our faith it is important for us to guard our minds from the things that will negatively impact our connection to Adonai.

"In other words, do not let yourselves be conformed to the standards of the *olam hazeh*. Instead, keep letting yourselves be transformed by the renewing of your minds; so that you will know what God wants and will agree that what he wants is good, satisfying and able to succeed" (*CJB*, Rom. 12:2). A mind that is conformed to the world cannot be under the transformation of the spirit of God. Allowing your mind to be wrapped in the standards of the world does two things, it draws you away from God then it pulls you closer to the adversary.

Paul admonishes the Philippians to " ...focus your thoughts on what is true, noble, righteous, pure, lovable or admirable, on some virtue or on something praiseworthy" (CJB, Phil. 4:8) and it's also applicable for us today. We can't focus on righteous thoughts or noble thoughts if our mind is inundated with unrighteous and ignoble thoughts. If we sit and watch 3-hours of a TV show that promotes promiscuity or witchcraft then bow before God seeking healing, do you think we are basking in the right spirit to imbue God's intervention? It just does not work.

The bible teaches us what is pure and what is lovable and righteous. Unrighteousness is everything that's contradictory to the word of God; everything that takes us off the path to God. God admonishes us against promiscuity, so the promiscuous reality show that we mark on our calendars to watch religiously is a perfect example of unrighteousness permeating our mind.

It's key for all of us to understand that Satan is constantly after us seeking any small opening he can exploit to draw us away from our Creator. He knows the mind is that opportune variable that if successfully exploited can yield disconnection from God. He knows if he attacks our bodies we will pray, fast and cry out more to God. Attacking our family members and friends will drive us to witness more, and it would give us a greater testimony of how great Adonai has been to us so that we can create more talmidim (disciples) for Yeshua. Creating contention at our jobs will just push us to commit more to the service of our congregations – maybe even driving us to full time mission work or into full time ministry. But successfully attacking our minds grants Satan the opportunity to influence how we speak, how we live, and ultimately how we perceive God. When we allow our minds to be renewed based on the standards of the world, we slowly begin to think evil is good and good is evil. Evil is not always bold and aggressively in our faces warning us to run. It can be subtle so that we get caught in the net of sin. These are the schemes of Satan.

The only way to guard against the mind attacks of Satan is to wear the helmet of salvation and the sword of the spirit which is the word of Elohim. The final verse I will close with is in Ephesians 6:10-17:

> Finally, be strong in the Lord and in his mighty power. Put on the full armor of God, so that you can take your stand against the devil's schemes. For our struggle is not against flesh and blood, but against the rulers, against the authorities, against the powers of this dark world and against the spiritual forces of evil in the heavenly realms. Therefore, put on the full armor of God, so that when the day of evil comes, you may be able to stand your ground, and after you have done everything, to stand. Stand firm then, with the belt of truth buckled around your waist, with the breastplate of righteousness in place, and with your feet fitted with the readiness that comes from the gospel of peace. In addition to all this, take up the shield of faith, with which you can extinguish all the flaming arrows of the evil one. <u>Take the helmet of salvation and the sword of the Spirit, which is the word of God</u> (*NIV*).

Remember, as believers we are called to be a light to a world that's filled with darkness. We must guard our minds and thoughts from the things of the enemy. The things of the enemy will prevent us from effectively walking faithfully with God and from being a testimony of light to the world.

WEEK 29 | ACTIVITY

What do you need to begin letting go of today to allow your mind to be freer to mediate on the things of God? Over the next week make a declaration list that outlines the things you plan to stop doing. Then follow-up with the list of things you will start doing to guard your mind from the things of the enemy. My prayer is that you will recognize the change in your connection to God after making the intentional effort to filter the things that you focus your mind on.

_____

_____

_____

_____

_____

_____

_____

_____

_____

_____

_____

_____

30

"WE SHOULD PROVIDE A GOOD TIP BEFORE LEAVING."

The Spiritual Message: Stand for righteousness.

You have heard it said that you should stand for what you believe in. On the surface, this sounds innocent. However, the problem with this statement is, if isolated from spiritual principles you risk the chance of standing for beliefs that completely contradicts the word of God. Look around your world, a lot of chaos exists because humanity has defined its own way and chose to hold it as right. In a room of ten people, you can find eleven different beliefs. At times, these different beliefs can be the harbingers for hate, discrimination, violence and wars.

The truth is the things we stand for should be grounded in the ways of God. The actions spewed from beliefs that are antithetical to God's word, are problematic. We must therefore fully understand the beliefs that we profess to believe in. Our beliefs really are moveable if they are rooted in anything but the foundation of Adonai's word. The better message is not to stand for what you believe in but stand for righteousness.

What is this righteousness that we should stand for? To expound, the word righteous is translated as *tsadiyq* in the Hebrew text. Righteous carries the concrete thought of being straight, or on target. Being straight here means to stay on God's set and direct path. So, staying on His straight path means you are walking out righteousness. Thus, we see David writes in Psalms 23:3 "He restores my soul; He guides me in the paths of righteousness for the sake of His name" (*NASB*). The Complete Jewish Bible (*CJB*) drives home the explicit meaning in its translation: "He guides me in right paths for the sake of his own name." Additionally, we see righteous still carrying the meaning for being straight, especially when paralleled with wickedness. In Psalms 37:17 It says, "For the arms of the wicked will be broken, but Adonai upholds the righteous" (*CJB*).

With the concrete understanding of what righteousness is, we should now be able to have a practical understanding of what it means to stand for righteousness. To stand for righteousness, we should be enthusiastically encouraging practices, thoughts, ideas, or behaviors that fall in line with being on the straight path; the paths that Adonai has laid out in His word. The paths in His word are the do's and don'ts He has carved out for us.

I remember many years ago being a young son in the faith, I had a memorable experience of someone who stood for righteousness. It was a Sabbath afternoon, post services, I was pulled to the side as I made my exit from the building looking to tarry home. It was my congregation elder that pulled me aside. My elder told me how concerned he was after hearing some news from his wife about me. He told me he heard that I wasn't being the most helpful to my mother. I remember him saying as a believer in Yah's word it should never be heard of me that I am not honoring my parents. For some this might have been the moment when they decided to stop serving in a congregation, or the moment they commenced a personal vendetta out of the perception of being attacked. Instead, it became a learning moment for me in how a believing community should encourage each other to stay on path. I know there might have been an expectation of a story where I talked about a saint standing in a line picketing for social justice, or a believer that sacrificed their paycheck to feed the homeless. And these all matter, however standing for righteousness permeates past the bounds of public good will, and very much crosses the path of being your brother and sister's keeper at a personal level.

My Elder on that sabbath afternoon stood for righteousness; he saw my faith and service weekly and knew that he needed to provide me that additional guidance to ensure I stayed on path and continued to grow in my walk with God.

We are 'heaven buddies' believe it or not. As heaven buddies our walk must entail a zeal to look out for each other and support each other in living the best life before the Father. Our personal mantra shouldn't be, "I know I am going to heaven and I know I have to give an account for myself so I care not for others". It should be the complete opposite. We should ensure we are on a straight path so that we can be an example and be a motivating voice for others.

Our life's purpose must be about being a conduit for others to accept Yeshua into their life, and to support our brothers and sisters to stay on path – the righteous path. That encounter with my congregational elder enlightened me that standing for righteousness is not a position about being a judge over anyone. The bigger picture is standing for righteousness means showing great love to each other by reminding our brothers and sisters how we should all stay on His path. This means we walk the path together and support each other in the journey to making it to eternity.

In culmination, standing for righteousness should be the mantra for all believers. We know we are doing this when we encourage practices, thoughts, ideas, or behaviors that falls in line with the path Adonai has laid out in His word. Standing for righteousness transcends just public display. Standing for righteousness is elevated when we are our brother's and sister's keepers – being great 'heaven buddies' by encouraging each other to be on that path of righteousness. I will leave you with the words of Yochanan (John), "anyone who does not practice righteousness is not of God, nor the one who does not love his brother and sister" (*CJB*, 1 John 3.10).

WEEK 30 | ACTIVITY

This week you get to create your *Heaven Buddy* list. Which family members, friends, or colleagues you wish to spend more time with going deeper into God's words and being a great support system to ensure you and those individuals stay on His path? Make that list, reach out and regularly check in on each other's lives weekly, bi-weekly, or monthly. You will be surprised how your daily experiences and journey can help to encourage someone in their walk with God.

_____

_____

_____

_____

_____

_____

_____

_____

_____

_____

_____

_____

31

"THERE'S A QUARREL OVER THE BILL."

The Spiritual Message: Seek peace.

*H*ave you ever asked yourself if the world could ever be a place of complete peace? Could you imagine existing on earth with no wars, genocide, or political rivalries? Rewind to the footage in your mind where a pageant contestant stood on stage and lamented on the need for world peace during the question-and-answer segment. We look at such responses as wishful thinking, right? And you are right, it is unrealistic for us to think the world would ever be in a state of complete peace without the presence of Yeshua himself. In Matthew 24:5-7 Yeshua said:

> Watch out! Don't let anyone fool you! For many will come in my name, saying, 'I am the Messiah!' and they will lead many astray. You will hear the noise of wars nearby and the news of wars far off; see to it that you don't become frightened. Such things must happen, but the end is yet to come. For peoples will fight each other, nations will fight each other, and there will be famines and earthquakes in various parts of the world (*CJB*).

Scripture clearly tells us wars and unrest will forever exist until Yeshua returns and sets up his everlasting kingdom. Yeshua, our salvation, is the only one that will grant us eternal peace.

Knowing the corruptible world we exist in will be unpeaceful until the Messiah returns, does that mean we as believers should have an expectation of unrest in our lives? In Romans 12:18, Rav Sha'ul (Paul) states "Repay no one evil for evil, but try to do what everyone regards as good. If possible, <u>and to the extent that it depends on you, live in peace with all people</u>" (*CJB*). This verse brings to mind the encounter between King David and Saul in second Samuel. Saul who formerly loved David later grew jealous of David's war success and sought to take David's life. During that ordeal David ultimately became a fugitive in exile in the wilderness of Ein-Gedi. While in Ein-Gedi Saul pursued David. However, in his pursuit, Saul made a military mistake by venturing out alone in the territory of his rival David. While Saul stood alone to relieve himself, David approached Saul secretly and cut off piece of Saul's robe. David had the opportunity to repay Saul's evil with evil; he could have easily killed Saul. Instead, David took the opportunity to show a sign of peace by sparing Saul's life. This example is quite the paragon of living in peace with all people, especially when we can influence the outcome. So based on Paul's words and from the example of David, we know that believers do have a role in promoting peace in the lives of ourselves and others despite the corruptible world we exist in.

All of us that are truly followers of Yeshua must understand that being conduits of peace is a requirement for the profession of our faith in Yeshua. On the Mount, Yeshua's words to the audience in Matthew 5:9 was, "Blessed are the peacemakers, for they will be called sons of God" (*NASB*). Then in 1 Peter 3:10-11 we read:

> The one who desires life, to love and see good days, Must keep his tongue from evil and his lips from speaking deceit. He must turn away from evil and do good; He must seek peace and pursue it (*NASB*).

All Those words show the compelling connection between peace and righteousness. Yeshua requires peace from those who will be called children of God, and we know only those that practice righteousness (*CJB*, 1 John 2:28-29) will be called His children.

Peter's words further outlines that the pursuit of peace, similar to shunning evil, is doing good. And we know doing good is righteousness. So, peace is equal to righteousness, therefore practicing peace must be a daily endeavor. Our mindset in avoiding missteps like stealing or lying and all other sins, must be the identical mindset to pursuing peace.

The final nugget to note is that in the scriptures peace really means wholesomeness or completeness. The corresponding Hebrew word used in the Biblical text for peace is *Shalom*. Thus, when we talk about soundness, safety, health, completeness or even a relationship with God, *Shalom* translates it all. Therefore, with this perspective we have a greater appreciation in understanding why peace as an element of the believer's walk is so important. Abandoning peace and not ensuing it means we are forsaking soundness, safety, health, completeness, and ultimately a covenant relationship with Adonai. Though the world turns in darkness and unrest, may those that are called by His name find Shalom.

WEEK 31 | ACTIVITY

What are the top ten things in your life causing unrest? It may be a person or situation causing this lack of peace in your life. Make a list of these items, is there anything you can do to fix the problem? If you have a direct path to influencing the problem, then move forward and begin to execute on solutions. If you have no direct influence over the issue, then here is where you have to offer it up to God. Worrying adds nothing to us, so we must lean in on God, trusting Him for the solution. As you engage in this week's activity utter these words of prayer as you seek God's guidance:

> *Dear Father,*
> *I ask for shalom, peace, to deal with this person(s) that are causing unrest for me. I ask you for shalom, peace to overcome this situation that is bringing unrest into my life. I offer up all my battles to you today. I have faith in you, the almighty living El, that you will grant me the peace that I desperately need in my life.*
> *Amein.*

_____

_____

_____

_____

_____

_____

_____

32

"I COULD NEVER ENVISION THEM ADDING NEW DRINKS TO THE MENU."

The Spiritual Message: We need His vision.

The most successful organizations in our world today have at least one thing in common, great vision. A great vision usually starts with a visionary leader who can look beyond the current state of their operations and look futuristically to a state in which their organization is more advanced. This can be either in their current market of operations, or in new markets. To memorialize the vision, a vision statement is created. The vision statement plainly states where the organization is going and how the organization will look once it gets to that desired state. It's basically setting the direction, or course, for where you want to be.

Having a vision is important, because if you do not have a prescribed direction then all available paths become yours – which ultimately means you will change paths often, and never reach your goals. The remarkable thing about this concept of vision statements and its importance to the corporate world is that this wisdom comes from God. The text in Proverbs 29:18 reads "Where there is no prophetic vision the people cast off restraint" (*ESV*). Or based on the King James Version, "where there is no vision, the people perish."

The wise words of Solomon means that a lack of vision yields a people that will essentially go astray. Though this text was referring to the detrimental outcome when there's no revelation of God's words and its meaning, there's a conceptual understanding that the lack of revelation comes with corresponding consequences - this is a concept that all believers can appreciate for living out their lives.

So, we recognize now that having a vision is important, now how do we make it practical? Vision in a western view relates to a self-evoking path that is derived from the seen or known. However, vision in a biblical context is celestially imbued, and stretches beyond the mere human thoughts, knowledge, or immediate understanding. Quite the contrast, isn't it, so what does that mean for you? That means if you are in search of the path you need to be on, desperately seeking a vision of where you should be, then based on scripture you can only turn to God for that answer. He is the only one who knows enough about the future to instill the insight.

I know this may sound superficial. You might ask yourself, "Do I bow in prayer then expect to be given an answer?" Well, here is where your faith and trust in Yeshua must grow. I recall the recount of Shlomo (Solomon) in 1 Kings 3. Solomon at about 12 years of age, obviously in doubt about his ability to lead given his youth and inexperience, prayed these words to Adonai:

> So now, ADONAI my God, you have made your servant king in the place of David my father; but I am a mere child — I don't know how to lead! Moreover, your servant is among your people, whom you chose, a great people so numerous that they cannot be counted. Therefore, give your servant an understanding heart able to administer justice to your people, so that I can discern between good and bad — for who is equal to judging this great people of yours? (*CJB*, 1 Kings 3.7-9).

What Solomon had said in making this request pleased Adonai. Solomon reached out to God for help, he sought after God to provide the understanding he needed to be successful in his role. Similarly in Exodus 3:11, Moshe's (Moses) words to Adonai was "Who am

I, that I should go to Pharaoh and lead the people of Isra'el out of Egypt" (*CJB*)? The theme of self-uncertainty is presented yet again; Moses inquires directly from Adonai for concrete guidance. In both examples God intervenes per Solomon and Moses' request. God answered their prayers by providing what they needed to direct the people of Israel. God's intervention allowed Moses and Solomon to fulfill the vision God had for His people.

Given this topic I think it's fitting to look at the words of James 4:2 "The reason you don't have is that you don't pray" (*CJB*)! If you can't cement your vision for this life, be it in ministry, your professional career, or in your academics, the answer to completing your vision is first found with prayer.

Prayer is the first step to sincerely invoke God's help to attain the vision He has for you. We are all here for His purpose. Therefore, if your purpose doesn't align with His, then that's your surest guarantee to a path of disaster. After you have prayed, your second step must be having an open heart to receive that direction. The direction may come from a direct word from God, through a familiar acquaintance, or from a stranger. You must be ready to accept that direction regardless of how unaligned you think that direction is to your personal feelings. Remember the words in Proverbs 3:5 "Trust in Adonai with all your heart and do not rely on your own understanding" (*CJB*). The third step is execution. When God has provided you the answer, you must have enough faith to move out and believe on His word. You must believe that what He has planned for you is the right path to be on. Many times, folks have clearly received the word of what they need to do, but due to doubt and fear they constantly turn in circles looking for more signs, or more clues. Remember faith without works is dead (*CJB*, James 2:26)! Move out on the vision God has given you and hold faith that He who has started a work in you will see it through to completion.

WEEK 32 | ACTIVITY

Are you ready to exercise your faith like Solomon and Moses? They prayed to God for a vision on how they were to lead the people of Israel. Likewise, if you are stagnant in your life and desperately need a vision from God; you are seeking guidance on your next move, then it's time to look to God for answers. Follow the steps outlined in this week's devotional, and trust God to provide the vision and guidance like He did in the past for so many believers.

For what are you seeking a vision? List them, then Pray, Receive, then Execute!

_____

_____

_____

_____

_____

_____

_____

_____

_____

_____

_____

_____

33

WEEK

"WOULDN'T BE GREAT IF WE GOT OUR MEAL FOR FREE?"

The Spiritual Message: We are afforded salvation for free!

*W*hen I was about ten years old, I attended a congregational picnic with my family. The day started with great laughter and joy. Everyone was having fun, eating, playing games, and engaging with one another. During that time, I decided to jump into the water. I remembered just goofing around in the water in an area where I could comfortably stand since I wasn't really a swimmer. Within a matter of seconds, I went from standing comfortably in the water to feeling as though someone pulled the earth from beneath me. Panic began to set in, and I recalled how the force of the sea pushed me farther away from the shore. The clear blue waters were now morphing into dark blue waters. At this point, my hands were swinging endlessly while I took what I thought would be the last look of all my friends and family enjoying life back at shore. But someone saved me. A family friend, an adult, was moving as fast as they could through the waters to rescue me. They grabbed me, held me, and pulled me back to shore. I was rescued by someone skilled enough to navigate the sea.

This was a frightful experience, one I wish to never repeat. However, the experience reminds me of how Yeshua rescued each and every one of us from drowning in the sea of sin. We were drifting in lawlessness so deep; the end was a physical and spiritual death that only the Adversary would find delight in. But Yeshua stretched out his hand and gave us life; He gave us eternal life so that we could dwell with him forever. This is the essence of salvation. The very meaning of Yeshua is salvation. Matthew 1:21 reads:" She will give birth to a son, and you are to name him Yeshua, [which means 'ADONAI saves,'] because he will save his people from their sins" (*CJB*).

Isn't it amazing to know that you have a chance at eternal life all because of what God sacrificed for us? I pen this message because I realize that many of us in our zeal to please God can sometimes get discouraged when we miss the mark. We commit ourselves to live a life of purity, being unstained by unrighteousness, but we fail at times erring to our disappointment. This can feel heavy because we feel as though our failure hurts our status with God. But the thing to remember here is, we did not work for salvation. Salvation is a gift given to us, for those who wish to accept it. So, once you have accepted his gift, then commit to his gift by following the instructions He has set out for us, that's all He desires. Certainly, we may have missteps, but Yeshua's wish is not that any will perish but that we would all receive eternal life. Our God isn't standing by waiting and hoping for us to mess up so that He can punish us. Humans may operate this way, but our God transcends typical human behavior.

I remember when I was younger, I once heard a minister say that there are some people in our world that have lost their chance of being save and there's no turning back to the light for them. It was very scary for me to hear those words. I envisioned being sent to hell without a chance of escape if I committed one more sin over the threshold. Can you imagine as a kid thinking that you would burn in fire all your life, because you lied, or stole one extra time over the limit? I know even as adults some of you certainly feel this way. I have heard statements such as, "God will never accept me for all I have done" and "I am doomed and learning to be alright with it." This message of damnation without repentance is certainly the message of the accuser – Satan. Satan attacks our thoughts and convinces us into believing we cannot be saved. Remember, this is not true! Yeshua didn't come down amongst us so His death would be in vain. Your walk to salvation is this simple:

> if you acknowledge publicly with your mouth that Yeshua is Lord and trust in your heart that God raised him from the dead, you will be delivered. For with the heart one goes on trusting and thus continues toward righteousness, while with the mouth one keeps on making public acknowledgement and thus continues toward deliverance. For the passage quoted says that everyone who rests his trust on him will not be humiliated (*CJB,* Romans 10.9-11).

Therefore, let no one deceive you, you have an open chance of salvation, so do not be discouraged or dismayed of your shortcomings. Seek forgiveness yes, but learn, move forward, and accept the free gift of salvation that God has offered you.

WEEK 33 | ACTIVITY

You might already have a good hold on your journey of salvation, but who in your personal circle do you know that needs God's salvation. Make a list of those individuals, then pray for a Paul like experience for them. In other words, pray that the scales be lifted off their eyes so that they may see Yeshua, and that they accept Him as their savior and begin to serve in His Kingdom.

If you are sure in your journey of salvation but have doubts at times in your walk, and you bear the attacks from the Adversary discouraging you, then ask God for bravery like Joshua. Look to God for strength and courage. Put the armor on over your mind and heart in order to resist the enemy and his lies. Spend time this week meditating on these verses: 2 Peter 3:9, John 3:16, John 6:40, Romans 10:13 and 1 Timothy 2:4.

_____

_____

_____

_____

_____

_____

_____

_____

_____

_____

WEEK 34

"I FEEL LESS DEPRESSED DURING BRUNCH."

The Spiritual Message: There's hope for the spiritually depressed.

Mental disorders are impacting our community today. There is a high probability that within any of our circle of friends or acquaintance groups, there is someone that is being impacted by a mental disorder. The tides of life are high enough to cover us, to the point that some of us drown under it. Drowning under life's gargantuan waves can be manifested through mental disorders such as clinical depression. The Mayo Clinic defines clinical depression as a mental disorder imprinted by a severe loss of interest in the most rudimentary activities of life, which then significantly impairs one's standard of living. I have seen relatives struggle with severe depression; there's just an air of sadness and melancholy regarding their outlook of life. Nothing matters to them; the world is a complete dark chamber without a hope of light. It sounds quite gloomy, doesn't it? I pen this piece on depression because I know there are people struggling with the physical realm of depression, but there's also the other weight of spiritual depression that many believers are facing.

Spiritual depression is that mood you consistently experience which detaches you from God. You have a low will to pray, a low will to worship, and a low will to be amongst the body of Messiah. It's a pit of spiritual darkness; a pit so deep the circular entrance can no longer be seen.

What got you to be spiritually depressed can be a myriad of things such as: burdens from the world's injustices, seeing evil things happen to innocent people, experiencing a heartbreaking loss or event in your life that left you feeling as though God has abandoned you, or a hurtful ending to a relationship with members of your congregation. These experiences are boulders that stop you in your journey in connecting closer to God. It's not your desire to be there, or dwell there forever. However, you find yourself farther away from God as you get detached from the things that are of Him. Now the question is, how do you break off the yolk of this spiritual depression and move back into a more fruitful relationship with God, the relationship that God really wants to experience with you. It may be difficult during your spiritual despair, but the effort that you must make is to fall into His word one more time.

In Psalms 143:7-8, David wrote in his despair these words: "Answer me quickly, Adonai, because my spirit is fainting. Don't hide your face from me, or I'll be like those who drop down into a pit. Make me hear of your love in the morning, because I rely on you. Make me know the way I should walk, because I entrust myself to you" (*CJB*).

Adonai is still available; He never left His role of looking out for you, His child. Like David, utter these words of help asking God to restore your faith. You should find confidence in the fact that we know how the story ends. David asked God to rescue him and lift his failing spirit, and we know God did rescue David from his despair. Since we know God is unchanging, you should have no doubt that the same God King David served is the same God you serve today. Therefore, crying out these words of rescue to God will get you the same result it did for David - The Adonai who comes in glory will lift your head, and pull you from the miry pit of spiritual despair.

Your mind as a major gateway to your spirit must also be guarded. As experiences occur that begin to or continue the thoughts of despair and abandonment, shun those thoughts by meditating on the words in Philippians 4:8:

Finally, brothers, whatever is true, whatever is honorable, whatever is just, whatever is pure, whatever is lovely, whatever is commendable, if there is any excellence, if there is anything worthy of praise, think about these things *(CJB)*.

Many times, our spiritual despair is molded by the information that's in the media, and various outlets that then feeds our minds. But remember, if you consume good your spirit will be nourished, but the more evil you consume your spirit will become malnourished. It's no different than consuming food – a pound of a healthy meal may add life, but a pound of an unhealthy meal will detract from your life. Cautiously consume good that will positively impact your spiritual health.

I close with these words from Romans 12:12, "Rejoice in your hope, be patient in your troubles, and continue steadfastly in prayer" *(CJB)*. The only way you can rejoice in hope, despite the troubles and despair you may face, is due to a mind that dwells on things that are spiritually uplifting. Never give up on God because he will not give up on you. Your experiences are par for the course. He understands. Find comfort in His word as he covers you through the storm you are experiencing. Be not spiritually dismayed, for He is with you.

WEEK 34 | ACTIVITY

What are the causes for your spiritual depression? Is it a congregation member? Is it an unanswered prayer? A shocking death in your personal circle? Try to dig within yourself to identify the situation that preceded the spiritual gloom you are feeling. If it's a person maybe here is a time where you can attempt to directly face this person and seek for reconciliation. If it's a situation, and it's one that you can change, then take the necessary steps to change it. A mindset focused on the positive and the higher meaning of our struggles is the first step to beating the depression attacks of the Adversary.

_____

_____

_____

_____

_____

_____

_____

_____

_____

_____

_____

35

WEEK

"PLEASE WAIT FOR THE SERVER."

The Spiritual Message: Remember authority is from God.

$\mathcal{M}$ost of us prefer living an independent life; we gravitate to circumstances that allows us to do exactly as we wish without control from others. Not too surprising, because every segment of our world is predicated on taking direction from someone, therefore we relish those spaces where we can make independent choices without the direction of an external party. From our youth through adulthood, we experience the various authoritative roles in our society. We entered this world then went through a series of days being nurtured by our parents, but soon after we learned there was an authority structure at home that was led by parents. Then, we stepped into the educational system and learned that the classrooms too had an authority structure of its own. We then grew to realize that regardless of where in life we stood authority always exists.

Well, authority exits throughout the fabric of our society because God instituted authority. From cover to cover of your bible you will read of God's establishment of authority. We read in Bereshit (Genesis) 1 the establishment of humans to rule over animals, then in Genesis 3:16 we see the family structure unfold – God told Chavah (Eve):

I will greatly increase your pain in childbirth. You will bring forth children in pain. Your desire will be toward your husband, but he will rule over you (*CJB*).

Though misquoted at times, Gen 3:16 in no way is meant to demean our women in society but is meant to merely lay out God's order. This order is described further in 1 Corinthians 11:3:

But I want you to understand that the head of every man is the Messiah, and the head of a wife is her husband, and the head of the Messiah is God (*CJB*).

Adonai our God is the ultimate ruler of the universe, and in His order, He placed His son Yeshua in charge. Then there are the fathers of our households, then there are the mothers of the household. But even outside of the familial structure God instituted authority to have a well-functioning society.

In Deuteronomy 16:18 we read of the appointment of judges within the Israelite community. These judges served as the authority to perform the righteous rulings needed to maintain the society. The text reads:

You are to appoint judges and officers for all your gates [in the cities] Adonai your God is giving you, tribe by tribe; and they are to judge the people with righteous judgment. You are not to distort justice or show favoritism, and you are not to accept a bribe, for a gift blinds the eyes of the wise and twists the words of even the upright. Justice, only justice, you must pursue; so that you will live and inherit the land Adonai your God is giving you (*CJB*).

Deuteronomy 20:9 shows this hierarchy structure again in the Israelite army, "When the officials have finished speaking with the soldiers, commanders are to be appointed to lead the army" (*CJB*).

The Israelite army was tiered with captains of thousands, hundreds, and fifties. This military structure we read of was purposefully instituted by God to position the Israelite army for success in battle.

The point here is that as believers we must remember that authority exists in our world because God instituted authority so that His creation can function in order, as He is an Elohim of order. But, with the deceiver Satan in the world, God's order is attacked through the spirit of rebellion. We as individuals may value our independence and the ability to be free, but as believers we must remember that we are not free to rebel against God's authority.

Rebellion is the resistance to authority, and all authority is from God. Romans 13:1-2 reads:

> Everyone is to obey the governing authorities. For there is no authority that is not from God, and the existing authorities have been placed where they are by God. Therefore, whoever resists the authorities is resisting what God has instituted; and those who resist will bring judgment on themselves (*CJB*).

Rav Sha'ul's (Paul) words in Romans 13 is a direct message to believers of Yeshua. Obeying the authority God has set to lead us is a direct acceptance to allowing Yeshua to lead you. The takeaway for those of us that are earnestly seeking to please the Father is that though we may not agree with our bosses at work, or our congregational leaders, or community leaders, they are set there for a purpose. Our behavior towards these women and men that have been placed in authoritative roles will impact our relationship with God. Let's not find ourselves guilty with the spirit of rebellion like the Adversary, who decided to rise against the ultimate authority and lead a rebellion against the Most High.

WEEK 35 | ACTIVITY

Our prayer this week is that God will imbue in us His spirit of humility that will enable us, as His vessels, to accept the authority He has placed in our lives. If there's an authoritative figure you have been struggling with accepting, find the time over the next seven days to seek God's wisdom to assist you in navigating this situation. Remember that our interactions with our authority is telling of our relationship with God. Everyday list those areas you will actively work on improving as you interact with this leader or authoritative figure. Is it your tone, speech, or behavior that will need to change going forward? Be precise on the areas you will be better at going forward.

_____

_____

_____

_____

_____

_____

_____

_____

_____

_____

36
WEEK

"PLEASE WAIT TO BE SEATED."

The Spiritual Message: Be patient.

℘arly in my professional career I had this great zeal to achieve more in my life. Due to my zeal for more I began searching for better employment. I applied for a role at an organization that was considered one of the most coveted companies to work for. Fortunately for me I got an interview. I was supper elated that I was being given the chance to get into this great company. It was no easy feat; I did a series of five interviews speaking with leaders from various parts of the organization. I also did personality tests, business cases, and mock presentations. The hiring process really felt like an extended iron man marathon.

Despite the laboriousness of the interview process, I placed complete faith and trust in God that He would provide a successful outcome for me. I prayed before going through the doors of the organization for the interviews; I believed what I was pursuing would be good for myself and my family. So, after saying my last intellectual words, and penning my follow-up notes of gratitude, it was time for me to wait for a response. After a few weeks I finally heard a response – I did not get the job. I felt so crushed knowing I had faith and placed my best foot forward, yet I didn't get the outcome I wanted. Utter disappointment plagued me along with the internal questions of why God didn't grant me this request.

But there is more. A few weeks after getting that disappointing phone call I received another call from the recruiter. The recruiter called to inform me that another hiring manager in the interview process was impressed with me. That hiring manager wanted me on his new team! Who knew this seemingly disappointing situation would have turned into one of the most exciting moments in my career?

After a few months of working in my new job then witnessing the personality and work dynamics of the role I got rejected for, I realized had I gotten hired on my first attempt I would have been displeased and unsuccessful in that role. The role I did get hired for turned into the exact career opportunity I needed to push forward into life.

The lesson here is that Adonai always knows what is best for us. Our short sightedness, need for speedy results, and tendencies to focus on the non-spiritual angles of this world can cloud our judgement. However, our all-knowing God, like a mother, cares for us His children and always has our best interest at heart, even beyond our own understanding. Since we can be sure that God is constantly working things out for our good, we must learn to be patient.

Isaiah 40:31 says: "But they that wait upon the Lord shall renew their strength; they shall mount up with wings as eagles; they shall run, and not be weary; and they shall walk, and not faint" (*KJV*). These words in Isaiah are more than just informing believers that they should wait on God, but it's a message to His people that waiting on God would yield benefits that would seem unnatural to the rest of the world. Who runs and never gets weary, and who walks endlessly without the desire to stop from fear of fainting? Waiting patiently on God, unlike waiting on other authorities in this world, would never lead to disappointment. Israel spent 430 years in Egypt before their deliverance came. Joshua and Israel circled Jericho seven days before their victory came. The woman with the issue of blood suffered for 12 years before Yeshua came and provided salvation and complete healing to her body. And even now, we all are waiting for the second return of our master Yeshua, the Mashiach – the Messiah. We know that His return will be the beginning to the greatest reward His followers could ever be patient for.

I know it's hard being patient in this world. We live in a world where speed, and quick results is the expectation. No one wants to wait for anything. One idiom says, "wait is a heavy load." But as you go through life you will learn that rushing into situations without the right due diligence leads to chaos. Remember, God is constantly looking out for your best interest. If you wait on God, we know the result will be an outcome that's for your good. Therefore, if we know He means good for us, we certainly need to rely on God and be patient!

WEEK 36 | ACTIVITY

Are you an impatient person? Have you been praying for a resolution to an issue that is yet to be answered? This week we remember the words in Isaiah 40:31, if you wait upon Adonai, He will come through for you. This week take a pause, be patient and trust God. Proclaim everything that you are being patient for from God. To bring life to this, jot down your proclamations. There's life in the number three, so take another step by writing these requests down three times. At the end of that part of the exercise, write a brief description of a person in the bible that waited on God for an answer or deliverance. This may require some research based on your familiarity with the bible, this is perfectly fine. Now based on that individual's walk with God, write two to three good qualities that person exhibited in their wait for deliverance that you can copy into your life.

_____

_____

_____

_____

_____

_____

_____

_____

_____

37

"WASH YOUR HANDS AFTER USE!"

The Spiritual Message: There're rewards for your obedience.

When I was younger there was a day when my dad picked me up from school then we stopped at a grocery store just before travelling to my aunt's house. Lying there just beside the handbrakes was a red knife that resembled a Swiss army knife. Before going into the store my dad warned me not to interfere with the knife. He cautioned me that the knife was extremely sharp, and that I could get hurt if I didn't listen to his instructions.

When my dad left the car, I stared at that red knife for 30 seconds before I decided to give in to the temptation of trying out the knife. I reached out to grab the knife, then I attempted to remove the blade from its base. It was quite difficult to remove the blade, so as you can imagine, I pulled harder to remove the blade. Well, the blade came out from its base covering, but my index finger was very close to the edge of the blade. Sure enough, my index finger got slashed by the sharp blade sending a shock of pain through my body. I was terrified by the cut on my finger because the wages of my disobedience were now apparent. I knew my father would be greatly upset.

My father returned to the car, and he quickly witnessed the cut on my finger. Needless to say, I got the punishment I deserved for clearly disobeying his orders. He wanted the best for me, he cared about my wellbeing, but I didn't recognize that well enough. Instead, I focused on giving in to my own will.

Like an earthly father, Adonai is our Av - our father. The Hebrew letters that comprise the word Av (אב) symbolizes strength and security. This is exactly what God is to us – our living all powerful God that protects and secures us. He loves us and desires nothing but the best for us His children. But like our earthly fathers that we disobey and rebel against, we disobey and rebel against God, despite He wants nothing but the best for us.

God has shown His interests in us by setting clear instructions for us to follow so that we can live a fulfilling life. But instead of following God's ways, like me with that red knife, we succumb to our own desires and neglect the instructions of God our father.

Obedience is a core ingredient to having a real connection with God. The obedience that God desires from us becomes a lot easier to comply with when we realize His instructions for our lives is not His way to control us, but His instructions are the way to lead us to three things: blessings, life, and salvation.

Obedience brings blessings. Deuteronomy 11:26-27 makes this clear: "See, I am setting before you today a blessing and a curse —the blessing, if you listen to the mitzvot of Adonai your God that I am giving you today" (*CJB*). Mitzvot are God's commandments, He makes it very clear that if you listen and obey his commands you will be rewarded with his blessings. Deuteronomy 28 further details these blessings we can experience in our lives due to our obedience. Here are a few from Deuteronomy 28: You will be given a great abundance, you will lend but have no need to borrow, your body will be healthy and fruitful, and you will be the head and not the tail. God's words are sure, He cannot lie, therefore we should feel confident that in our obedience God will fulfill His promise to us.

Obedience brings life. Ephesians 6:1-3 reads:

> Children, what you should do in union with the Lord
> is obey your parents, for this is right. Honor your
> father and mother — this is the first commandment

that embodies a promise — so that it may go well with
you, and you may live long in the Land (*CJB*).

Earlier I stated that God is our heavenly father, and like a good
earthly father that cares and protects His children, so too is our God.
Well, the vertical structure with parents and children that exists in a
household embodies the heavenlies. Therefore, disobedience to our
earthly fathers and mothers is disobedience to our heavenly Father.
And the converse is true, obedience to our earthly father and mother
is also obedience to our heavenly Father. Obedience will grant us
physical life! If you have any doubt, reference God's interaction
with Solomon when he became king: "if you will live according to
my ways, obeying my laws and mitzvot like your father David, I
will give you a long life" (*CJB*,1 Kings 3.14). Our obedience to our
creator influences the type, and length of life we live while we walk
this earth.

Obedience yields blessings and life, but most importantly,
obedience leads to salvation. We do not attain salvation because we
completed a list of defined tasks, we can never do enough to earn
the right to save our self. Paul reminds us of this in Ephesians 2:8,
"For you have been delivered by grace through trusting, and even
this is not your accomplishment but God's gift" (*CJB*). God gives
us a choice to accept His gift of salvation. Once we have accepted
His gift then it's ours. However, those that have chosen to accept His
gift of salvation must show that they have truly accepted His gift by
walking in God's ways.

Hebrews 5:9 says: "And having been perfected, He became the
source of eternal salvation for all those who <u>obey</u> Him" (*NASB*).
Further, Yeshua tells us clearly in Matthew 7:21-23 that those who
go against his commandments, laws or instructions will not enter
into heaven:

> Not everyone who says to me, 'Lord, Lord!' will enter
> the Kingdom of Heaven, only those who do what my
> Father in heaven wants. On that Day, many will say to

me, 'Lord, Lord! Didn't we prophesy in your name? Didn't we expel demons in your name? Didn't we perform many miracles in your name?' Then I will tell them to their faces, 'I never knew you! Get away from me, you workers of lawlessness!' (*CJB*).

Obedience is a core ingredient to having a real relationship with God. The relationship that yields blessings, life, and salvation. Our obedience to God is not a situation of mere subjects serving a dictator, it's more so a quintessential love story. A love story of a great and awesome Av, our father, that wishes to grant us all that we desire, and in return He only asks that we obey His voice, because this shows that we love Him in return.

WEEK 37 | ACTIVITY

Obedience matters. A sound relationship with our Father is dependent on our willingness to listen and obey His voice. What message from God have you been ignoring? These messages or direction could be directly from the Father, through His word or even His messengers. Your conscience is honest, so you know when you have neglected the voice of God. I challenge you this week to reflect on what you have disobeyed, then focus on how you can change course to align yourself with what He has asked of you. Obedience is a reflection of your faith. If you trust and believe that God's words are just, then you should always feel confident that your obedience to Him supersedes the outcome you get when you go your own way.

_____

_____

_____

_____

_____

_____

_____

_____

_____

_____

38

"THEY DEFINITELY MISSED THE MARK ON THIS MEAL!"

The Spiritual Message: Missing the mark impedes our connection to God.

One of my favorite cardio workouts is playing basketball at my local gym. The whole point of the game of basketball is to score as many points as possible to outpace your opponent. The team that ends with the most points win the game. The game is fairly straightforward. However, the challenge is being able to score a point. To score a point you apply art in holding the ball away from your opponent, then aiming towards the basketball rim, while keenly focusing on placing the right amount of strength to then shoot the ball so that it falls through the basket. Most amateur and even professional players will tell you that in a game, every shot will not land in the basket. We all wish for 100% efficiency when shooting the basketball, but in reality, it doesn't happen. When you shoot the ball and it doesn't fall through the basket, the ball likely bounced off the back of the board, or hit the rim, or was probably an air-ball because it hit nothing and fell straight to the ground. These are all considered misses. Anything less than the ball going through the net is considered missing the mark.

Missing the mark reminds me of sin, because the meaning of sin is to miss the mark. We may think that the concept of sin is very abstract and differs from congregation to congregation, or person to person. But in fact, just like how a missed shot in basketball is universal, so too is the concept of sin. Realizing what sin is sets us up as believers to recognize the things we should be avoiding so that sin, or the concept of missing the mark, does not impede on a fruitful relationship with our Creator.

The word for sin in the Hebrew text is translated as *hhatah* (חטאה). It carries the meaning of missing the goal or target. That word is evident in passages like Leviticus 4:1-3:

> Then the LORD spoke to Moses, saying, "Speak to the sons of Israel, saying, 'If a person sins unintentionally in any of the things which the LORD has commanded not to be done, and commits any of them, if the anointed priest sins so as to bring guilt on the people, then he is to offer to the LORD a bull without defect as a sin offering for his sin which he has committed (*NASB*).

So re-translated, a person that missed the mark in following the instructions that God has commanded needed to provide an offering – an intentional act of acknowledgement and repentance for missing the mark. But what's the target that once missed is considered sin? As seen in the text, the target is God's instructions or commands.

Folks at times paint commands with a negative connotation. But in fact, every segment of our society including our homes are governed by do's and don'ts. Even the game of basketball has guidelines that its players have to follow. Likewise, God who gave us His breath to walk this path of life has provided the best instructions for us to live out a blessed life. Whose instructions are better to follow than our heavenly Father, who we know without a shadow of doubt loves us. Following God's instructions can never be burdensome, His instructions are exactly the guides that will ensure we live our best life.

In Genesis 3 we read the account of sin amongst mankind. First, we understand that mankind was living in close contact with God, dwelling with the Creator. God bestowed great power upon them, allowing them to rule over all living things. However, He gave them just one instruction. He gave the specific instruction to not eat from the tree in the middle of the garden, but mankind ignored God's instruction and ate of the tree. The result was a severed relationship with God. God pronounced them with curses due to their disobedience, then He sent them out the garden away from His direct presence.

To this day we all bear a major suffering from the first sin: lack of a perfect relationship with God. The perfect relationship with God is where we can see God face to face, *panim el panim*. This perfect relationship will only be restored post the end of this corrupt world when we join Yeshua and the Father. In this present day though, we can experience the presence of God in our lives through His Ruach – His Spirit. These connected moments with God that we relish are sacred and precious. Our connectedness to Him breathes life that transcends just the physical – it empowers our mind, hearts, soul and spiritual being. Hence, when we sin, we hamper that bond of connection with the Father. Isaiah 59:1-2 calls this out for us:

> ADONAI's arm is not too short to save, nor is his ear too dull to hear. Rather, it is your own crimes that separate you from your God; your sins have hidden his face from you, so that he doesn't hear (*CJB*).

If you are praying and crying out to God yet it feels like He is so far from you, then maybe it's time to look within yourself by doing an introspection of where you may be missing the mark.

The great news in all of this is that even though we may miss the mark sometimes, we have a path to correcting it – we have repentance! Yes, sinning is bad. However, failing to repent is far worse. Failing to repent shows pride, and self-governance, these are of the spirit of the anti-messiah.

In culmination, remember that every player steps on to the court hoping to be 100% efficient in scoring. In reality it doesn't happen. They shoot a shot up and it may miss the mark, but as important as shooting is, remember rebounding is as important. The best players shoot then rebound their miss, then they attempt another shot for a successful score. This is a direct analog to us as believers and sin. We may miss the mark in our attempt to be flawless in following God's instructions, but similarly we must have the same persistence to seek repentance from God when we do stray from the path of His instructions. Our relationship with God is at its best when we truly know His instructions, when we follow them, and when we repent from missing the mark. May we all experience the best and purest relationship there is to experience with God while we dwell on this earth.

WEEK 38 | ACTIVITY

Today, let's say these words in prayer: "Dear Abba, Father. We repent from missing your mark. We repent from falling short of the standards you have set for us. We know we have the ability to be all that you expect of us, therefore we want to do our best so that you can say well done my servant. Please forgive us of our missteps today. Amein."

The best way to communicate your shortcomings is in prayer to the Father. Taking personal time for prayer can never be underestimated. But realize that our prayers are hindered when we live a life short of His expectations. That's why it's always important to seek His forgiveness as often as we can.

Knowing this, reflect on the things that are causing you to miss His mark. Go through this week identifying these repeat offenders that causes you to miss the mark. After you have identified these culprits, make the commitment to omit these culprits from your life. You may stumble on this journey, but you can be successful!

_____

_____

_____

_____

_____

_____

_____

_____

39

"TELL ME THE TRUTH, WOULD YOU EAT HERE AGAIN?"

The Spiritual Message: Honesty matters.

*A*cts 5 opens up with these words:

> But there was a man named Hananyah who, with his wife Shappirah, sold some property and, with his wife's knowledge, withheld some of the proceeds for himself; although he did bring the rest to the emissaries. Then Kefa said, "Why has the Adversary so filled your heart that you lie to the Ruach HaKodesh and keep back some of the money you received for the land? Before you sold it, the property was yours; and after you sold it, the money was yours to use as you pleased. So what made you decide to do such a thing? You have lied not to human beings but to God!" (*CJB*)

Here in Acts 5 Paul recounts the deceit perpetrated by a couple considered part of the believing community. You can see from the text that the couple had no apparent reason to lie, yet they did. For their actions their ultimate wage was death. The text went on to say: "On hearing these words, Hananyah fell down dead; and everyone who heard about it was terrified. The young men got up, wrapped his body in a shroud, carried him out and buried him" (*CJB*).

Paul notes that everyone that heard of the incident was terrified. I was terrified too when I first read this scripture. I remember hearing this story of Hananyah and Shappirah (Ananias and Sapphira) as a lad. Hearing that story left me completely terrified to know that my life could be directly removed by God due to my dishonesty. This scripture highlighted for me the severe consequences of dishonesty.

One question some ask is, so a merciful God will kill me just for being dishonest? The crux of Hananyah and Shappirah's sin was not the mere issue of altering the truth, the grander issue is the lack of fear of God. Deuteronomy 6:24 reads: "ADONAI ordered us to observe all these laws, to fear ADONAI our God, always for our own good, so that he might keep us alive, as we are today" (*CJB*). In essence, the moment we decide to go about our own way, like doing all the things that are contrary to God's ways – like practicing falsehood as seen in Acts 5, it is at that moment we show lack of fear to God. This is to say we are our independent unit, with greater knowledge, knowing better than God himself.

The adjective honest, as used in the bible, denotes straightness. One of the Hebrew words used is yosher (יֹשֶׁר). Yosher drives the meaning of rightness or uprightness; be it in the measure of practicing equity, measures of weight or being trustworthy. The point is honesty for believers is exemplified in doing all upright actions. Some biblical examples are not being a false witness, being trustworthy, and of course a bearer of truth. And notice that honesty is not solely about you as an individual providing the truth for yourself, but it extends to your neighbor! Being fair and equitable to others or being *upright* in support for another human that is being wrongfully hurt or accused, is part of the measure in exemplifying honesty.

Another note for us is that we must recognize that our measure of honesty is also a measure of our faith. If we don't believe God will deliver us, we will try to solve the problem ourselves, which usually includes the worse tactics. Here are some examples of tactics with Abraham and Isaac. In Genesis 20, "Abraham journeyed on to the region of the Negeb, where he settled between Kadesh and Shur. While he resided in Gerar as an alien, Abraham said of his wife Sarah, She is my sister. So Abimelech, king of Gerar, sent and took Sarah. But God came to Abimelech in a dream one night and said to him: You are about to die because of the woman you have taken, for she has a husband. Abimelech, who had not approached her, said: O Lord, would you kill an innocent man? Was he not the one who told me, 'She is my sister'? She herself also stated, 'He is my brother.' I acted with pure heart and with clean hands." (*NASB*). Also, in Genesis 26 we see a similar example. Isaac given his fear of the people in Gerar, he altered the truth about Rebekah being his wife. Despite God specifically told Isaac he should go down to Gerar, a direct sign of God's guidance on Isaac's life, Isaac relied on his own tactics to face the Philistines.

One of the lessons the two examples relay is the lesson on honesty and faith. When we don't trust God enough to fulfill His promises to us, like protecting us, or providing for us, we then lean on our own strength and understanding. It is at that moment we rely on mere fleshly devices like dishonesty to get our desired short-term needs.

To honor the long-standing dictum on honesty, I will say honesty is not only the best policy, but it's also God's policy. We must constantly remind ourselves that God has called us into a life of purity, which will entail shedding dishonest behaviors. We see from scripture, that the practice of dishonesty will yield only detrimental consequences in this world and the next. Moreover, we should understand that if our faith and trust truly rest on God, we should not fear. Adonai will provide our every need; we have no reason to dwell in dishonesty. Let us all be straight and upright following the example of He who died for us, Yeshua HaMashiach (Jesus the Messiah).

WEEK 39 | ACTIVITY

Honesty is a reflection of our faith. If we truly believe we are His, then we should never have to practice dishonesty for personal gain. What has caused you to be dishonest recently? Does your answer to that question unveil a situation in which you were low in faith? You might realize there's a trend where every dishonest situation is connected to an episode of low faith. You didn't have faith that God would reveal himself and work on the heart of the person you had to share news to, or you didn't have faith God would open a door of opportunity for you just the way you are. The list can go on. If that trend exists for you, this week, focus on beginning to believe more in God. Know that you can have faith in Him for every situation, so you have no need to lean on your own devices.

40

WEEK

"I'M LOVING THIS CELEBRATORY BRUNCH!"

The Spiritual Message: It's ok to rejoice.

All my life I have never been overly ecstatic over anything, the exception would be the birth of my daughter and getting married to my beautiful wife. Usually, I have a stoic reaction to the attainment of major milestones in my life. I have never had the type of excitement like Tom Cruise's iconic image jumping hysterically on top of Oprah Winfrey's sofa. Through the major milestones of graduating university on time, making it through grad school, having gainful employment, landing a six-figure income, or even owning multiple properties, I always celebrated those milestones with the question of what's now ahead. Certainly, I was grateful, I know I travailed a great deal to make it to those accomplishments. But I knew very well that each one of those accomplishments were direct blessings from God himself. I shunned overt happiness or joy, because I equated an abundance of happiness and pride to these accomplishments as a revocation to the acknowledgment of God's direct intervention in my life. Interestingly, I spent more time rejoicing during my lowest moments. I would give thanks that the situation wasn't worse and found the space to rejoice over what was going well. As mind bogging as this may sound, this was truly my concept on rejoicing for years in my life.

Clearly, my concept on rejoicing was flawed; it's the example you wouldn't memorialize for your youth convention. One day I was listening to a minister speak on the radio as I drove home from work, the minister said something that stood out to me at that moment. He asked the rhetorical question, if you can't rejoice when God blesses you why do you think He would bestow further blessings upon you? All this time I never thought to put rejoicing in this context. It finally struck that rejoicing should be less about me and my image of humility, and more so about an action that acknowledges true gratitude for the blessings from God. I immediately asked God for forgiveness; though I thought I was grateful, my forfeiture of rejoicing for His blessings was contrary to what He expected of me.

When turning through the scriptures we see numerous cases of our forefathers of the faith setting great examples on the lesson in rejoicing. For me, the embodiment of rejoicing must be King David. In 2 Samuel 6:14-15 we read how David rejoiced to the returning of the Ark of the Covenant to Jerusalem:

And David was dancing before the LORD with all his strength, and David was wearing a linen ephod. So David and all the house of Israel were bringing up the ark of the LORD with joyful shouting and the sound of the trumpet (*NASB*).

This was David rejoicing before God in the streets as they entered through the city. I have the mental image of David just spinning in circles with arms wide open moving through the streets giving his best shouts to Adonai. I earnestly believe this is the stellar example of how we should rejoice before God given His blessings upon us. We should freely sing, dance, and shout before God without care of what anyone else would say about us or caring about how we look rejoicing.

For all that God has done for us, we should rejoice. I have since applied this lesson to my life, learning to rejoice in both the great times and not so great times. As Paul said in Philippians 4:4 "Rejoice in the Lord always; again I will say, rejoice" (*NASB*)! Whether in suffering or in wealth, learning to rejoice with abandon before YHWH sets us in a place, like King David, to having a heart after God.

In fact, I believe the very importance of rejoicing is underlined by the number of words that is used to translate rejoicing in the biblical text. In English there are but few words for rejoice, however the bible carries over 16 Hebrew words for rejoice! One translation is *gil* (גִּיל), this is rejoicing that embodies spinning around in a circle. This is the same image I had of David rejoicing in the streets before Adonai!

The point here is this, sometimes it's hard for us to rejoice. It could be due to the difficulties of life that we are enduring, or we exist in this base state of emotion. This base state of emotion can be due to past experiences that causes us to think that something bad is always about to happen. Instead, we need to understand rejoicing is one of our tools to put the adversary at bay. It's our weapon to show HaSatan he has no hold on us, therefore we should rejoice both in the good times and the bad.

Recognize that rejoicing is not your revocation of humility. When we receive blessings in this life, those of humble minds at times think reflecting joy is a sign of excessive pride. But it isn't. I have now learned that you can and should rejoice in the blessings that have been bestowed upon you, they are from Yah above – this is your sign to God that you are grateful for His blessings. Do not underestimate your response to God's mercy and blessing towards you. Rejoice!

WEEK 40 | ACTIVITY

I know God has done great things for every one of us. If we were to list all the great things we should rejoice for, we would run out of paper. So today, we don't have to list all, but what are twenty things God has done for you in the last twelve months that you would like to rejoice over. Write them down then find the time to celebrate in your own way to acknowledge how great God has been to you.

_____

_____

_____

_____

_____

_____

_____

_____

_____

_____

_____

_____

41

WEEK

"THE SERVICE HERE WASN'T GOOD."

The Spiritual Message: Always give your best to God.

$\mathcal{O}$ne day, I indulged in a late morning breakfast while sitting a few feet away from my daughter who was attending virtual school due to the COVID-19 pandemic. As I sipped on my now lukewarm tea, I overheard the teacher providing, what I would call, concise instructions to the virtual class specifying the steps needed to complete the math assignment for the day. When the teacher finished giving the instructions for the assignments, there were a few minutes of silence. The silence was interrupted by a student who raised a question to the teacher. The student asked the teacher, "What if I can't complete this assignment?" My ears instantly perked up in anticipation of the teacher's response. The teacher then nobly responded, "Do your best, all I have ever asked of you is that you do your best, do your very best." In that moment I thought about how that child received that response. There are many ways that teacher could have responded. She could have been dismissive, or completely ignore the child, or unempathetically guided the child to complete the work. But to me her words were direct, personal, and sincere; sincere in a way that made the child self-examine what is truly their best.

After hearing the teacher's response, I could not help but think how analogous the situation with the teacher and the student is with God and us. God has told us that His yolk is easy and his burden is light. All that He requests of us isn't as far as the heavens so we can't attain it, or deep below the seas so we can't reach for it. His word is near and close to us so we can receive it and do it. All He has ever wanted from us is for us to give completely of our hearts and serve Him, giving Him our best.

The words in Matthew 25:21 are the words many of us are hoping Yeshua will say of us: "Well done, thou good and faithful servant: thou hast been faithful over a few things, I will make thee ruler over many things: enter thou into the joy of thy lord" (*KJV*). In its context the Master is rewarding the servant who was prudent with the resources that was given to him; the servant gave the best of himself to please his Master. Are you like the faithful servant, are you doing your best with all that has been bestowed to you? If Yeshua was to visibly show himself to you right now wherever you are at, are you confident that if He asked are you doing your best you would be able to reply confidently with a yes?

Giving your best is more than the tithes or offerings you give to your place of worship. You might have heard congregational leaders taunt the words give your best offering, but our best to Adonai supersedes legal tender. Giving your best to Adonai is predicated on additional variables that creates the complete believer. Giving your best to Adonai entails 1) your commitment to study His word, 2) using your talents for God, and 3) giving of your time and resources to help other believers and non-believers.

A commitment to indulge in Adonai's written words is a tenet of us as believers giving our best. You see, it's easy to go to service for a few hours once or twice a week then re-escape into the world of social media, excessive web searching or money chasing. But what takes a bit more effort, is long after the last teaching or sermon is made, or the last song is sang, is engaging in personal time with God by reading His word line upon line daily. 2 Timothy 2:15 teaches us to: "Study to shew thyself approved unto God, a workman that needeth not to be ashamed, rightly dividing the word of truth" (*KJV*). We also see this theme in Acts 17:11:

> Now these people were more noble-minded than those
> in Thessalonica, for they received the word with great
> eagerness, examining the Scriptures daily to see
> whether these things were so (*NASB*).

The word eager translated from the Greek word *prothymia* also means zeal! What happens when you are zealous after something? When you are zealous for something you give your utmost best! So, like the Berean believers in Acts 17 who gave God their best through their commitment to study the scriptures, so to must we. Our zeal in studying the scriptures is a direct representation of us giving our best to Adonai.

The second tenet that shows us as believers giving our best is the use of our talents. I am one of those that think I have no special talent on most days, but in actuality, we all have been given a gift. Our gifts can and should be used for the Kingdom of Elohim. Romans 12:6-8 reads:

> But we have differing gifts meant to be used according
> to the grace that has been given to us. If your gift is
> prophecy, use it to the extent of your trust; if it is
> serving, use it to serve; if you are a teacher, use your
> gift in teaching; if you are a counselor, use your gift
> to comfort and exhort; if you are someone who gives,
> do it simply and generously; if you are in a position of
> leadership, lead with diligence and zeal; if you are one
> who does acts of mercy, do them cheerfully (*CJB*).

The moment we decide to hold on to our talents and not use it for God, then we have shortchanged Him. Giving our best to God conveys using the talent that He has given us for the building up of His ministry; the spreading of the good news – the *besorah* of Yeshua.

The final tenet to show how we give our best to Adonai is through the act known as love.

"Rabbi, which of the mitzvot in the Torah is the most important?" He told him, "'You are to love Adonai your God with all your heart and with all your soul and with all your strength. This is the greatest and most important mitzvah. And a second is similar to it, 'You are to love your neighbor as yourself.' All of the Torah and the Prophets are dependent on these two mitzvot" (*CJB*, Matt. 22.36-40).

I highlight loving your neighbor as a true tenet, because once you can show that you love those who you see, that in turn means you love God (1 John 4.20). Copying the words of admonition from Peter, "More than anything, keep loving each other actively; because love covers many sins" (*CJB,* 1 Pet. 4.8). Showing love to others through various acts of supporting the poor, the fatherless, the widow and destitute amongst us, is a direct depiction of a believer giving their best to Yahweh Avinu (God our Father).

I will leave you with these words, we give our employers our best, we give our academics our best, we give our relationships our best, but what do we give to God? God gives us the best therefore we should give Him our best. The way we give God our best extends beyond money. Our best to God entails the time we take to study and understand his written word, it entails the time we take to not just attend our congregational services, but to serve in the body by giving a helping hand through our gifts and talents. Our best entails the love we show to humanity, because our love to humanity is a symbol of our love to God. Remember, your service to God here on earth is a shadow of your service in eternity.

WEEK 41 | ACTIVITY

This week we identified ways we give our best to God, namely studying the scriptures, giving our talents in service to the Kingdom, and showing love to humanity. As you look forward to the days ahead try to grow in the above tenets of giving your best. Set at least one hour every weekend to study God's word. Close your door, place your phone on silent mode so that you can close off all distractions of the world. I guarantee, as you engage in this you will realize one hour is not enough time, before you know it you will be spending multiple hours just digging into the holy writ.

What about your talents? Return to the reading of Romans 12. Whatever you feel blessed to do, get the mentorship or guidance from your congregational leader to begin doing your talents at your congregation. If you struggle with identifying this, take the time to pray to God to ask that this be revealed to you. You can also confide in a close friend to have them provide insights to you about the thing or things they recognize you are good at. Your talent is more obvious than you realize.

And don't forget to show love to everyone you encounter. Helping others and looking out for those in need are some of the ways you can show your love.

_____

_____

_____

_____

_____

_____

42

WEEK

"FORGIVE ME FOR SPILLING YOUR COFFEE!"

The Spiritual Message: God is merciful.

One day as a kid I heard a preacher lament, "there will come a point when God stops reaching out after we fail to beckon to his call; this will be the point of no return, the point where we will be lost forever". That statement made me shake and shiver. Every slip up I made thereafter made me wonder if I finally reached that threshold where God will turn his back on me and no longer extend His mercy.

The image I had of God, based on that minister's message, set the tone for my relationship with God that was based on perfect fear instead of perfect love. I have grown and since learned that God can be the Father that chastises, as good ones do, and still be the Father that rewards us with great health, wealth, and prosperity. What's important to note is that He does all this based on our actions, our own choices. If we do evil, then our reward is commensurate with evil. If we do good, our reward is commensurate with good. But through it all, one thing we can attest to is God's wish is not that any of us would perish, but that we would all have eternal life. What this tells me is that Adonai is not lurking in a corner wishing for us to misstep so He can wipe us out of His book. Instead, Adonai is merciful, He wants to extend His mercy towards us.

One of the words used to translate mercy into the Hebrew language is the word *Rachamin*. Rachamin is based on the root word rechem, which means womb. When you think of the womb what feelings or emotions surface for you? The womb is symbolic of the most noble connection you can find in life, which is the connection between a mother and her child. Notice that before the mother witnesses that first strand of hair, or the color of the eyes of that child, an unbreakable bond and love already exists between the two. The mother has an unconditional love, and compassion towards the child. While in the womb, the child unable to feed themselves relies on the loving mother that provides all the nutrition the child needs. That connection from the womb is the harbinger for the unconditional love the mother holds for the child. This is the same connection that allows a mother to have a heart that always looks to forgive their child. With God it's no different! God has an extended line of mercy and compassion to each and every one of us.

Psalms 119:156 tells us "Great are Your mercies, LORD," or according to the original manuscripts, MANY are your mercies (*NASB*). The use of the word 'many' connotes an unmeasurable count of mercies that have no end – it's infinite. And in Hebrews 4:16 we read: "Therefore, let us confidently approach the throne from which God gives grace, so that we may receive mercy and find grace in our time of need" (*CJB*). Doesn't this sound like a God that is willing to pour out His mercies upon us? 1 John 1:9 further reminds us that "If we acknowledge our sins, then, since He is trustworthy and just, He will forgive them and purify us from all wrongdoing" (*CJB)*. The words in 1 John 1:9 aren't words that should ignite fear that causes us to wallow in a relationship that resembles subjects and their dictator. Instead, these words should affirm how compassionate the God we serve really is, He's our Av HaRachamim – The Father of Mercy.

I will impart these final words, many of us have experienced this deep sadness and remorse for sins we have committed, wrongs we have made, and it eats at us. There are just somethings we wished we never did. We then wonder if God who is so good could ever take us back or forgive us for our evils. But God loves us so much. He wants to extend mercy to us, no matter what we have done; this is the God we serve. It is important for us to know this and accept His mercy. Therefore, no matter what state we are in, we should come before God, seek His face, and seek His forgiveness, because He is willing and able to forgive all those that seek repentance.

WEEK 42 | ACTIVITY

As a mother is to her child, merciful and compassionate, so is God to us His children. Whatever is eating away at your spirit my prayer for you is that you will release it and let God show His mercy towards you. You are never too far gone for God to reach out and bring you into His boat of salvation.

Also realize as God is merciful to you, you too must be merciful to others. The same way we receive we must give. This week, relish on the words in Hebrews 4:16. Seek God for anything you wish to repent of. And once you have released it in prayer, make a promise to yourself to never revisit this burden. Then secondly, think about any individual that is seeking your mercy and grace because of something they did to you. Here is your chance to provide mercy. The mercy you will give will be a great release for the person, but it will be an even bigger release for you!

43

"THIS IS NOT WHAT I ORDERED!"

*The Spiritual Message: Good things happen to bad
people, and bad things happen to good people.*

Why do bad things happen to good people? This is a question
that's often asked, especially during discussions on the validity of
God. If you ask five spiritual leaders this question you would get
five different responses. But here is my response that I wish for you
to think about. When we ask why do bad things happen to good
people what are our standards of good and bad? Who do we consider
good or bad? Who is your perfect example of a good person and
who is your perfect example of bad person? If we ask this question
using our human rubric, then I'm not sure of the response. Because
amongst ourselves we classify good and bad differently. The person
our neighbor considers good our friends may call bad. And to the
contrary, the person our friends call good our neighbor may call bad.
But guess whose rubric of good and bad is certainly objective? God's
rubric of good and bad is objective. Now you may wish not to accept
it, that's your free choice to do so, but that does not negate the fact
that in His word He has categorized what is good from what is bad,
or who is good from who is bad.

I believe instead of asking why bad things happen to good
people, the more appropriate question to ask from a more spiritual
perspective is why do evil happen to the righteous. I believe His word

gives us answers to these seemingly complex questions. From His word, here are three reasons why righteous people experience evil. Righteous people experience evil because 1) Sin exists 2) HaSatan aims to destroy those that are not his – the righteous 3) The life of the righteous is a story/forerunner for others salvation. Let's explore these in more detail.

Sin Exists

You can recount in Genesis 2 we read of the unveiling of sin into this world. The serpent tempted Eve or Chavah to eat of the fruit, she in turn gave it to her husband who also ate. Due to their breaking of God's command all humanity became cursed, thus existing in a sinful world now waiting for Yeshua's second return to put a complete end to sin. Here is where the tape should quickly rewind to the last statement I made – we exist in a sinful world *waiting* for Yeshua's return. Sin exists today, and why does that matter? It matters because where there is sin there is imperfection. That means there is untimely and wrongful deaths, sickness, lameness, famine, and dangerous natural disasters. Essentially everything that is the antithesis of heaven, the perfect state, exists here on earth the imperfect state. So regardless of whether you are righteous or unrighteous, based on God's standards, we all share space in this sinful and imperfect world. Remember Matthew 5:45, Yeshua's words were: " ...For he makes his sunshine on good and bad people alike, and he sends rain to the righteous and the unrighteous alike" (*CJB*).

Matthew 5:45 in its right context is really talking about God's love to all humanity, He provides blessings to all of us despite we are good or bad. But what we can also deduce from these words is the God who shares His bounty of rain and sunshine to all peoples, when He stops the rain and sunshine, He does that for all humanity as well. Both the righteous and unrighteous will experience those tribulations, just like in the time of Elijah when no rain fell in Israel for 3 ½ years. There was still a remnant of righteous people in Israel, yet they experienced the drought too. Tribulations will be part of the experience for the Tzedek, the righteous. Remember it was Yeshua that said, "In the world you have tribulation, but take courage; I have overcome the world" (*CJB*, John 16.33). What does these tribulations entail? Maybe the sudden loss of loved ones, a severe sickness, or even a catastrophic financial loss. There's a flood of items that meets the category of tribulations. But what is important to understand is that we will experience these things, even though we are righteous. Prior to entering the gate of His Kingdom, we must endure through this sinful world.

HaSatan Seeks To Destroy Those That Are Not His – The Righteous

We can recall the experience of Job, a man that was considered upright. Satan, the Adversary, sought to persecute Job because he believed Job would turn against God if he endured enough persecution. Let's revisit what the text says:

> Now there was a day when the sons of God came to present themselves before the LORD, and Satan also came among them. The LORD said to Satan, "From where do you come?" Then Satan answered the LORD and said, "From roaming about on the earth and walking around on it." The LORD said to Satan, "Have you considered My servant Job? For there is no one like him on the earth, a blameless and upright man, fearing God and turning away from evil." Then Satan answered the LORD, "Does Job fear God for nothing? Have You not made a hedge about him and his house and all that he has, on every side? You have blessed the work of his hands, and his possessions have increased in the land. But put forth Your hand now and touch all that he has; he will surely curse You to Your face." Then the LORD said to Satan, "Behold, all that he has is in your power, only do not

put forth your hand on him." So Satan departed from
the presence of the LORD (*NASB*, Job 1.6-12).

From the text it is clear that Satan is not on our side, unlike God
whose will is not that any of us would perish but that we have eternal
life, Satan's goal is the complete opposite. The goal of the Adversary
is that he brings as many of us into eternal damnation. In his effort
to win souls to hell, he attacks those that walk in the way of Yeshua
to rob them of eternity with God. This is what Job experienced.
Job endured a great deal of evil at the hands of Satan. Job lost his
wealth, his children, and his health. Yet through it all he did not sin
nor blame God (Job 1:22). Therefore, if you wonder why, you as a
righteous person, are facing certain calamities in your life, or why, a
person you observe as righteous is being plagued with great evils, you
should meditate on the experience of Job and strengthen your faith.
Realize that you have been so pleasing to God that Satan is terrified
of you, he has set his sights on your life so that he can rob you of the
prize of eternity.

Your Life is A Story

Matthew 5:14-16 leads with: "You are light for the world. A town
built on a hill cannot be hidden. Likewise, when people light a lamp,
they don't cover it with a bowl but put it on a lampstand, so that it
shines for everyone in the house. In the same way, let your light shine
before people, so that they may see the good things you do and praise
your Father in heaven" (*CJB*).

Your experience as one that is righteous serves as a testament
to others to the glory of Adonai. Think about someone that suffered
through tribulations, probably some of the worst experiences any
human can think of. But then think about how God brought them
from their tribulation to being triumphant. From our scriptures
Joseph is one that perfectly meets this caption. What did Joseph do
to his brothers to receive that mistreatment? He was certainly an
obedient son, analogous to righteous followers and God their father.

Yet in his obedience what happened to him? Joseph, sold into Egypt, experienced a string of misfortunes though he staid faithful to God. At the end of it all did you notice how God raised him up to be a deliver for all the nation of Israel? The experiences we question as evil happening to the righteous can also be for His design to deliver someone, or a group of people.

The experience of Joseph was a shadow of the Messiah, Yeshua! So, when you think about righteous people enduring evil, like Joseph, also think of our greatest example, Yeshua HaMashiach. Yeshua is the ultimate benchmark of righteousness, he had no sin in him: "You know that he appeared in order to take away sins, and that there is no sin in him" (*CJB*, 1 John 3.5). As perfectly righteous as Yeshua was on earth, He bore beatings and ultimately a crucifixion - the most cursed way a Jew like himself could die (Deu 21.23). But the crucial thing we understand from His experience is that, like Joseph, He went through all of that so He could grant salvation to us all!

A great lesson for us as righteous followers of our teacher, Rabbi Yeshua, is that our personal experiences are part of a larger chasm. Your personal experience can be that one situation that presents the opportunity for someone to turn to God, and your personal experience can be that opportunity for the world to see how powerful and awesome God is!

In culmination, I understand that it is never joyous for us as a people to go through the evils and tribulations this world has to offer. We look upon ourselves or others then ask why do the righteous experience evil. But remember even Yeshua who was all righteous experienced evil. Therefore, the lesson for us is that we must understand our experience as righteous followers are not without cause, they are for a purpose, they are ultimately for His purpose. Whenever we question our battles may we reflect and take to heart the words in 2 Thessalonians 5:16-18: "Always be joyful. Pray regularly. In everything give thanks, for this is what God wants from you who are united with the Messiah Yeshua" (*CJB*).

WEEK 43 | ACTIVITY

We can fall into the trap of questioning God for our experiences, but remind yourself that you do not know more than God does. We are not fairer than He is. And we are certainly not more righteous than He is. Therefore, we must trust and have faith in Him. If you are struggling in a situation that you are experiencing that seems unfair to you, engage in this exercise. Imagine if you had 60 minutes to talk to God face-to-face, what are all the questions you would ask Him regarding the experience you are facing right now? List the questions. After you have listed the questions, next to each question you would ask, write a comment about how the experience underlying each question could bring glory to God. I am not sure what questions you may have, but you will find if you take a moment to pause and think on every situation, you will find there are many ways God can get the glory and be praised out of the situation.

> *Dear Abba Father,*
> *We may not always know the reasons why things happen the way they do, but we trust in your perfect knowledge that you know the best for us. We accept the path that you have laid before us. We accept all that you will do in our lives, you are all good. Forgive us for questioning you. Grant us perfect peace so that we can walk boldly with our heads high knowing that we walk in your ways, so come what may, we will be covered under your arms.*
> *Amein.*

_____

_____

_____

_____

44

"I THINK I MIGHT GRAB BRUNCH ALONE NEXT WEEK."

The Spiritual Message: We find strength from alone time with God.

*D*uring one of my alone moments, I sat in my comfy chair, with my eyes glued to the computer screen, and my headphones tucked over my ears while I crunched through some financial models. While taking in the backdrop of great worship music I ploughed through my work on the computer. During the course of listening to music a song, *Here in Your Presence written by Jonathan Egan,* caused me to pause from the work I was focused on. It's a fortunate thing no one will hear me sing the words, you'll get to save the mirrors in your home. But the words from the verse and chorus are: *"Found in Your hands Fullness of joy, Every fear suddenly wiped away, Here in Your presence All of my gains now fade away, Every crown no longer on display. Here in Your presence. Here in Your presence, We are undone, Here in Your presence, Heaven and Earth become one, Here in Your presence, All things are new, Here in Your presence, Everything bows before You."*

Hearing the words from that song brought a sense of peace upon me. Sure, the music composition was great, however it's more about what the words helped to inspire for me. At that moment spirituality was no longer just a backdrop behind my work, at that moment the need to connect with God was front and center for me. My alone

176

time to do extra work for my corporation became my one-on-one time with God.

To be in a place where I could absorb the presence of God meant I needed to shun the distractions of everything else in my life so that I could focus solely on God and truly have an experience where I could be in His presence. The question to us all is, how often are we able to truly detach ourselves from the world and allow for the quiet time to solely focus on God?

Rabbi Jesus is our greatest example of the need for quiet time to focus on God. In Luke 5, after Yeshua healed the lepers from their ailment, He went to a quiet place to find time with God:

> But the news about Yeshua kept spreading all the more, so that huge crowds would gather to listen and be healed of their sicknesses. However, he made a practice of withdrawing to remote places in order to pray (*CJB*).

Again in Mark 1 we see Yeshua carving out alone time to connect with the Father: "Very early in the morning, while it was still dark, Yeshua got up, left, went away to a lonely spot and stayed there praying" (*CJB*, Mark 1.35) If Yeshua our perfect example did this daily, then surely, we understand nothing less is expected of us.

The quiet times when we aren't bombarded with the media and the gossip on social platforms, are the times when God's words can penetrate the noise around us. His words can provide the daily guidance and strength we need to get through our sicknesses, our worries, our financial shortcomings, and our relationship battles. The most beautiful thing about seeking God's presence is that He wants to be amongst us. Though our inferiority to Him is beyond human measurement, He loves us that much that He too wants to spend time with us, His creation.

In Genesis 3:8 we read, "They heard the voice of Adonai, God, walking in the garden at the time of the evening breeze, so the man and his wife hid themselves from the presence of Adonai, God, among the trees in the garden" (*CJB*). Some may read this verse and get wrapped up in Adam and Eve's state post sin, but what I want to exhume here is the fact that God's presence was desiring to be amongst them, but they made the decision to forfeit the opportunity to be in God's presence. The Hebrew word for *walk* used in the text is the word *halak*. You see, *halak* carries the connotation of not just merely walking with one foot after the other, it carries the meaning of walking, while moving intimately hand-in-hand with another person. So, in Genesis 3:8, the text is hinting to us that prior to Adam and Eve's sin it was customary for them to engage in these intimate, hand-in-hand walks with God. This means that those of us who are willing to draw near to God can experience a semblance of this if we shut out the sinful distractions in our life and create the quite space to commune with God.

Most of us, if not all, have set one-on-one times with our bosses. We discuss with them our progress on projects, obstacles we are encountering, job progression we would like to attain, and the list goes on. In our non-spiritual life, we recognize the need for one-on-one time with our leaders. Well, similarly, one-on-one time to just drown in the presence of God is also needed.

Though there are many reasons why the distractions of this world can get the best of us, let's remember that the only way we can overcome the problems in this world, and overcome the fears, is to draw close to God. Then, and only then, will we be able to sing like Jonathan Egan "in your presence we have found fullness of joy and every fear is suddenly wiped away!"

WEEK 44 | ACTIVITY

You just read the importance of alone time with God. If this isn't something you have scheduled as a regular part of your life, then commence that this week. Set a hard and fast time that you will commit to communing with God daily. Go as far as placing this time on your electronic calendar on your phone, computer, or whichever electronic device you use often. Spend at least 30 minutes praying, talking, singing, or just mediating on God's word. I guarantee that this will yield benefits in your life that you didn't experience in the past.

_____

_____

_____

_____

_____

_____

_____

_____

_____

_____

_____

_____

_____

45

"THE QUICHE LOOKS GOOD; I SHOULD HAVE ORDERED THAT QUICHE INSTEAD."

The Spiritual Message: Avoid envy.

It's a typical Monday morning in a kindergarten class, there is group of boys playing, and one has the latest hot wheels car. During their play session, one of the boys began to fuss about not having enough time with the brand-new Hot Wheels car. The older Hot Wheels car caused no issues in the past, but as soon as the new shinier car was added, a flare happened between the boys.

I think we are all guilty of this, we see the new and flashy things in life then we get the urge to have that new flashy item. We call this envy. We tend to have envious feelings for our neighbor's nicer lawn, we are envious for the prettier house, and even envious of our friend's vacation experiences.

I have certainly been guilty of envy in the past, but I was reminded of Paul's words in Galatians 5:19-21:

> Now the deeds of the flesh are evident, which are: sexual immorality, impurity, indecent behavior, idolatry, witchcraft, hostilities, strife, jealousy, outbursts of anger, selfish ambition, dissensions, factions, envy, drunkenness, carousing, and things like these, of which I forewarn you, just as I have

forewarned you, that those who practice such things
will not inherit the kingdom of God (*NASB*).

Paul's words make it clear that envious behavior should never be
part of the way of believers. However, we sometimes find ourselves
in this entrapment.

Whenever you are tempted with envy think of yourself as someone
with a swollen red face. The word for envy used in the Old Testament,
or better described as the Tanakh, is the word *qin'ah* – which means
to redden. Another definition for envy based on the word *qin'ah*, is
to burst with pain for that which belongs to someone else. None of
us would like to acknowledge our envy is that appalling right? But
based on the image of a red swollen face, this is exactly the visual
representation of what it means to walk around with an envious spirit.

My belief is that allowing envy to promulgate in us is a clear
denial to our trust in God. What is it that we are need of that God
cannot provide? What makes us think we must wish for another
person's things? All that we need God can provide, so we should
never let our wants of this world overtake our lives to the point of
envy. Proverbs 23:17 advises us: "Don't envy sinners, but follow
the example of those who always fear God; for then you will have a
future; what you hope for will not be cut off" (*CJB*).

Based on Proverbs 23, I deduce that our hearts should not be in
a place of envy, instead our hearts should be in a place of zeal for
the things of God. They say there's a thin line between love and
hate but there's also a thin line between envy and zeal. Both carry
the connotation of passion; the difference is zeal is a passion for the
things of Adonai.

When I think more about zeal and envy, Elisha and Joseph's
brothers come to mind. Joseph's brothers envied him for his dreams
of future rulership, whereas Elisha had a zeal to serve God the way
Elijah served God. Therefore, before Elijah's earthly departure,
Elisha told Elijah "Please! Let a double share of your spirit be on
me" (*CJB*, 2 Kings 2.9)! Elisha's words to Elijah exemplifies what

was meant in Proverbs 23:17 with the words follow the example of those who fear God.

My final note is this, it's quite fine to have great zeal after the things of God, whereas it's not as okay to envy the material things in this world. It's okay to have a zeal to worship Adonai like the vocalist on your worship team, it's okay to have a zeal to dissect the word like that fellow Rabbi or pastor, and it's definitely okay to have that zeal to be a servant to many as Yeshua was. A zeal for righteousness, instead of envy for unrighteousness, is part of the recipe to draw us closer to God.

WEEK 45 | ACTIVITY

Our envy reflects our level of faith and trust in God. If our heavenly Father can provide all that we need, why do we need to burst with envy for the things of others? This week let's focus on our thoughts and actions towards others when they move about with their material things. Every time you are tempted with those thoughts that are envious, remind yourself that those that are His lacks nothing! Write that statement out if it helps you feel reassured. God provides, so you have no need to burst in envy for the things of others.

_____

_____

_____

_____

_____

_____

_____

_____

_____

_____

_____

46

"BE CAREFUL, THE COFFEE IS HOT!"

*The Spiritual Message: Death stings, but fear
not because God conquered death.*

When I was growing up I heard of death due to the death of older people. However, death didn't resonate with me. Death was nothing more than attending a funeral event with my parents. My experience with death changed when I lost my father.

I lost my father when I was 21 years old. I felt like life would go on forever, but at that moment when I experienced familial loss, I realized death was something that could hit anyone at any age, without any warning. I no longer felt invincible after losing my father. Every death I heard of thereafter felt so close to home. It seemed as though more people I knew were just dying. This experience took such a toll on me that I began to have anxiety. Almost every day I woke up I felt as though it would be my last day on earth. I really felt like this was it, today would be the day I die from a heart attack. This anxiety was so real for me that I began having chest pains and tingling in my arms.

Reading this might sound so foreign and insane to you, and it's fine if it does. Our experiences and interaction with death will be different, but the important lesson from this that I am most interested in sharing is the lesson of acceptance. In one form or the other we will all encounter death. The question is, knowing this fact that death will come, what do we do while we have life?

I told you about my personal bout with anxiety, which was caused by my fear of death due to the loss of my father who died relatively young. However, the good ending to my experience is that due to the prayers of my mother and God's Ruach on my life, I overcame my fear of death.

Delving into God's word will show you that the true believer is one that understands death has no hold over you. Hear Yeshua's words to Martha in John 11:21-26:

> Marta said to Yeshua, "Lord, if you had been here, my brother would not have died. Even now I know that whatever you ask of God, God will give you." Yeshua said to her, "Your brother will rise again." Marta said, "I know that he will rise again at the Resurrection on the Last Day." Yeshua said to her, "I AM the Resurrection and the Life! Whoever puts his trust in me will live, even if he dies; and everyone living and trusting in me will never die. Do you believe this" (*CJB*)?

How powerful are these words from our Mashiach (Messiah)? We know we will face the first death, call that the standard, but our joy and anticipation is for the second life where we will live without the presence of death! In that new life we will have no pains or sickness, or fatal viruses. Why should our joy rest in a world that's plagued with evil, injustice, and sickness? Our hope must be for that new Jerusalem where we will live in mansions with Yeshua!

Remember Yeshua died too, He experienced a gruesome death; quite frankly a death that none of us will ever experience. However, we have the promise that if we accept Yeshua and walk in His ways, we get the opportunity to dwell with Him. Understand that our earthly death is just the beginning of a new chapter: "It will take but a moment, the blink of an eye, at the final shofar (Trumpet). For the shofar will sound, and the dead will be raised to live forever, and we too will be changed" (*CJB*, 1 Cor. 15.52). This my friends is the new chapter we are all looking forward to!

So, instead of having anxiety or fear of the death that we all can and will experience, our focus should be on living. Our focus must be on living our life to serve Adonai according to His ways. Remember to love, show compassion to all you encounter, and carry out the things God has asked us to do. The real death we should fear is the second death, the death where there is no return or possibility of resurrection.

Remember, God has conquered death, so we as His children should not fear. We are only passing through this realm looking onwards to the new world with our Father. Be of good cheer, Adonai is with you and will always be!

WEEK 46 | ACTIVITY

Death stings, but God has conquered death. We have the hope of eternal life through Yeshua's death. If you are experiencing a lull because of a personal experience with death, I hope you can find comfort in the promise of Yeshua's return. He promised we will be raised and spend eternity with Him. This is a promise we can hold to and believe in with all confidence. This week instead of focusing on death, let's focus on life. What are the things you can look forward to in the upcoming year if your life exists? List at least seven things you want to look forward to. Now focus on embarking on these journeys, experiences, or goals. Keep living, there's a lot more life in store for you until His return.

_____

_____

_____

_____

_____

_____

_____

_____

_____

47

WEEK

"NEXT WEEK, I WILL BRING MY DAUGHTER TO BRUNCH."

The Spiritual Message: Teach our children His ways.

*E*very one of us started this life as a young lad being cared for and natured to maturity. After years of seeing our parents raise us, we are now in the shoes that our parents filled, we are parenting children of our own. We might not have all had awesome parents, but the fact is we are now parents holding responsibility for the greatest heritage there is. What we do in our titles as mothers and fathers is highly important. We have a serious responsibility, not just as parents, but as believers to raise and do right by the children in our care. So how do we do right by the children in our care?

Proverbs 22:3 shares this message with us: "Train a child in the way he [should] go; and, even when old, he will not swerve from it" (*CJB*). In Proverbs 22:3 the word *train* is translated from the Hebrew word *hanak. Hanak* is said to be based on an Israelite custom. The custom was that amongst the mid-wives, they would teach the newborns how to suck by getting chewed dates then rubbing it all over the newborns' palate. This custom with the Israelite mid-wives and the newborns embosses the meaning behind training a child. In other words, we can connect training a child to providing a fruitful life for our children. Training a child in the right way is a matter of life and death. So, given the criticality of raising our children the right way, what is really the right way you may ask?

Let's look at Hannah as an example of training a child in the right way. In 1 Samuel 1 we read:

> Now when she had weaned him, she took him up with her, with a three-year-old bull, one ephah of flour, and a jug of wine, and brought him to the house of the Lord in Shiloh, although the child was young. Then they slaughtered the bull and brought the boy to Eli. And she said, "Pardon me, my lord! As your soul lives, my lord, I am the woman who stood here beside you, praying to the Lord. For this boy I prayed, and the Lord has granted me my request which I asked of Him. [28] So I have also dedicated him to the Lord as long as he lives, he is dedicated to the Lord. And he worshiped the Lord there (*NASB*).

As you know, Samuel grew up following all the instructions of Adonai, judging Israel, and prophesying to His people. He is the apotheosis of growing up under the direction of God.

Now, our kids may not be dedicated to serve in the temple today, but from the recount of Samuel's calling, what we can gather is that raising our children the right way means having our children follow all the ordinances Adonai has set forth in His word, and not departing from it.

In Deuteronomy 5, Moses repeats the ten commandments for all Israel to hear, he also goes on to remind Israel that following God's commands yields rewards like long life and prosperity in the land. Then, in the subsequent chapter, Moses gives a short podcast on how believing parents should raise their children. He said:

> Hear, Israel! The Lord is our God, the Lord is one! And you shall love the Lord your God with all your heart and with all your soul and with all your strength.

These words, which I am commanding you today, shall be on your heart. And you shall repeat them diligently to your sons and speak of them when you sit in your house, when you walk on the road, when you lie down, and when you get up (*NASB*, Deut. 6.4-7).

There it is an explicit action on how we as parents should raise our children. We are to teach them God's ways; we should teach them His commands every opportunity we get so that His word becomes engrained in their hearts and minds so that they will never depart from it!

Adonai has given us the perfect guidebook on how we should raise great sons and daughters for His kingdom. My bet is once you carryout Adonai's instructions as seen in Deuteronomy 6, you will stave off disaster from your children; disaster that engulfs so much of our young people today. Our society is filled with all sorts of ungodly ideologies that overwhelm the educational institutions and platforms many of our children interact with. These ideologies have placed even more pressure on us as parents to steer our children away from the work of the Adversary. We will be tried even more as we get closer to the coming of Yeshua our Messiah. Despite the pressures we face, find comfort in the fact that God's words never return void, God will take care of our children. By doing His ways and teaching them to our children, we are setting them up for a blessing!

WEEK 47 | ACTIVITY

As busy adults it can be very difficult to set aside time to focus on all the things you would like to do with your child. These impressionable years are finite, therefore as hard as it seems, you must find the time to spend quality moments teaching them the ways of God. If you have children, or if you are instrumental in the life of a child, stay committed over the next four weeks by carving out at least an hour every week to do an activity with them that's centered on connecting with God. Make the time about developing a bond with them, while connecting with God. You can play games, do art activities, or engage in anything that brings life and meaning to understanding faith and learning the ways of our Creator. Don't treat this time as another moment that needs to pass by but treat this as a moment that fulfills Deuteronomy 6. It's a time to nurture your child and spend quality time together. Make a list of activities you can engage in then do a different activity each week.

_____

_____

_____

_____

_____

_____

_____

_____

48

"DO YOU WANT YOUR DISH SERVED COLD?"

The Spiritual Message: Revenge is God's.

The bible is the perfect guide showing us exactly the best way to live our lives. But let's be honest there are some directions in the bible that some of us struggle with keeping or adhering to. One major biblical principle that I think most of us struggle with is how to address revenge. Some of the most popular movies are the ones centered on revenge. We feel connected to those plots that are based on a victim returning havoc to their victimizer. We have a sense of affinity with the victim who repays the wrong done to them. No surprise movies like Taken, Kill Bill and even John Wick grabs our attention as we see evil being repaid. Those action movies reveal what most people dream of doing to the folks that wronged them. But is this the right approach to deal with those that wronged us?

In Romans 12:17 we read:

> Never repay evil for evil to anyone. Respect what is right in the sight of all people. If possible, so far as it depends on you, be at peace with all people. Never take your own revenge, beloved, but leave room for the wrath of God, for it is written: "VENGEANCE IS MINE, I WILL REPAY," says the Lord (*NASB*).

Also, in Proverbs 24:29, King Shlomo's (Solomon) wisdom was "Don't say, I'll do to him what he did to me, I'll pay him back what his deeds deserve" (CJB). And for a third witness from the scriptures, Proverbs 20:22 reads "Don't say, I'll pay back evil for evil; wait for Adonai to save you" (*CJB*).

These scriptures send a message that's the opposite of what we see in our revenge movies. God's intent for humanity is not that we rage wars destroying each other and being perpetrators of evil. Because of our choices, we now have a society that's filled with the cycle of revenge.

Unlike man, Adonai sees the heart and can apply the appropriate mercy in every situation due to His celestial understanding of a person's life. When we leave the act of revenge in God's hands, we avoid wrongfully hurting others that are undeserving.

Another note worth mentioning on revenge is the fact that God has specific revenge guidelines. In His word God crisply lays out what should happen when someone faults another person. For example, in Exodus 22, we read about the restitution for stealing and negligence. This is a passage you should take the time to read. The guidelines in Exodus 22 are all God's wisdom on how a society should be run.

Another reference worth noting is Numbers 35. In Numbers 35 Adonai gives the structure for dealing with murder. Realize these cases were not independent decisions by victims within the community of Israel, instead there were Tribal judges, or the Sanhedrin, reviewing these cases amongst the community then applying God's laws to exact the appropriate judgement. This may sound like our current day court system.

Now imagine, if unlike the court system, we all took the streets executing revenge based on our own way, based on our own thoughts. It would be utter mayhem, probably a semblance of the Purge. No two humans would exact the same type of revenge for the same evil. This is the reason God wants us to submit to Him for revenge, instead of submitting to ourselves.

God knows that there's a time and place for everything. He understands when war is needed, He understands when a punishment is needed, He knows when peace is needed (Ecclesiastes 3). We must lean on God's wisdom to fight our battles. Allowing God to fight our battles is really a deep expression of our faith. Allowing God to fight our battles is the way we profess to God that we trust him enough to keep His word to protect us from all harm and danger, and to exact judgement according to His understanding. We should certainly trust that God will always be fair.

I know, it's hard. You wish to get even with that person, I totally understand. But ask yourself this. If given the chance, how would you exact the deserved punishment on this person you think deserves it? Judgement and revenge have always been based on God's wisdom. Leaving revenge to God is not necessarily a mystical directive. God shows up for us in many forms. He shows up through others, in the hearts of our accusers, or through His direct intervention.

I will leave you with these words. Moses encouraged the children of Israel when they were fleeing from Egypt. Moses told them: "The LORD will fight for you, while you keep silent" (*NASB,* Exod. 14.14). These words are still true for the body of believers in this generation today. Amein.

WEEK 48 | ACTIVITY

Today my prayer for you is that the peace, or Shalom from God, fills you so that any pain you are carrying because someone hurt you may subside. The passion you have now to repay evil to someone that wronged you, may it be quenched through the peace of Yeshua.

This week make a note of every person that you are holding in your heart to exact revenge. Then next to each person's name list the emotions that surface when you mention their name. Cry this through if you need to, scream if you need to, shout if you must. But release the pain through your emotions. The last step is to run a line through each person's name and the corresponding emotion they raise in you. Then put the note "I am leaving it to God."

I know it looks like this is just an exercise on paper, however this exercise will carry a lasting change in your life. Through this exercise you will eliminate your drive for revenge but ignite your passion to let God work on your behalf.

_____

_____

_____

_____

_____

_____

_____

_____

49

"THIS FOOD REMINDS ME OF A GOOD WORSHIP SERVICE."

The Spiritual Message: God loves our worship!

*H*ave you ever wondered what it means to worship God? If you attended a worship service recently, you might have heard the worship leader or vocalist say words like "Let's worship the Lord!" And if you listen to contemporary worship artists, they use the same words in their songs. It's almost like a staple line in their records. But when you hear those words, what call to action is ignited for you? Is it to lift your hands, is it to sing louder? I am certain if we did a survey amongst believers, we would get various answers pertaining to the true meaning of worship.

Worshiping God is ultimately about Him, not us. I believe that much we can agree on. Consequently, like a spouse who wants to be treated a particular way, so too does God desire a particular way to be worshipped. He desires a much different way than the way people worship their worthless gods, or their earthly things, or their celebrities and fragile human heroes. Some worship their earthly gods through mutilating their bodies, or through other perverse practices. There are numerous ways the secular world engages in worship. But we know our God is unlike any other, so to please Him we should desire to understand how He wants us to worship Him.

In Exodus 4:13, the scriptures recount one of the early interactions the children of Israel experienced with God:

> Then Moshe and Aharon went and gathered together all the leaders of the people of Isra'el. Aharon said everything ADONAI had told Moshe, who then performed the signs for the people to see. The people believed; when they heard that ADONAI had remembered the people of Isra'el and seen how they were oppressed, they bowed their heads and worshipped (*CJB*).

Then in Joshua 5:13 we read of Joshua's interaction with one of the Melachim (Angels):

> One day, when Y'hoshua was there by Yericho, he raised his eyes and looked; and in front of him stood a man with his drawn sword in his hand. Y'hoshua went over to him and asked him, "Are you on our side or on the side of our enemies?" "No," he replied, "but I am the commander of ADONAI's army; I have come just now." Y'hoshua fell down with his face to the ground and worshipped him, then asked, "What does my lord have to say to his servant?" (*CJB*).

In the recounts of Israel and Joshua we observed that both worship experiences were associated with some part of their body in a downward position. Well, the word worship used in the above verses is translated from the Hebrew word שחה, transliterated as *shahhah*. *Shahhah* in its truest meaning refers to bowing down or prostrating oneself. It carries the connotation of the ultimate reverence a person can give to someone. *Shahhah* depicts the inferior being presenting themselves in a humble state without personal pride as a subject to the superior being. This is the very essence of worship to God. Worship to God involves our denunciation of self and ego, and a declaration to subject ourselves physically in a humble form by bowing down to God.

The image of worship should remind you of Paul's words in Philippians 2:9-11 talking about Yeshua:

> Therefore, God raised him to the highest place and gave him the name above every name; that in honor of the name given Yeshua, <u>every knee will bow</u> — in heaven, on earth and under the earth — and every tongue will acknowledge that Yeshua the Messiah is Adonai — to the glory of God the Father (*CJB*).

On that Day we know we will all worship Him the way He wants, which is to prostrate ourselves in humility and reverence before him. This topic on worship matters because if we are preparing ourselves for His return we must, with zeal, bask in the things that we know Yeshua desires of us. If we can't worship Him the way he wants now, what makes us think we can worship him the way He desires in the coming Kingdom? Now is the time when we all must get our hearts, mind and souls ready. We get ready now by worshipping God His way – bowing before him, subjecting all of ourselves to Him. Yes, singing, dancing, and shouting songs of praises certainly shows our adoration and thanksgiving to the creator. But true worship to God, the one that we all will do in His coming kingdom, resembles us bowing and falling on our face before the King of Kings, Yeshua HaMashiach (Jesus the Messiah).

WEEK 49 | ACTIVITY

Worship doesn't have to be in a congregated setting, your worship can happen with just you and God. I believe the real breakthrough moments in our life occur when we are by ourselves seeking God. So as part of your personal time with God, it's good to incorporate moments to worship. My hope is that this is an act you can begin doing starting from today. Take at least 15 minutes, at least one day a week to do this. Practice the act of prostrating fully before God, this is our act of full submission, and humility. By prostrating yourself you will see that worshipping before God brings to light the real meaning behind God lifts up the humble. If you bow, and worship before God, He will lift you up to overcome all that is before you.

50

"HE'LL PROBABLY STRAY FROM THE GROUP AFTER BRUNCH."

The Spiritual Message: God hurts when we stray.

*O*ne of the most impactful experiences I had when I was a teen, was being uprooted from my home country. I had to say goodbye to all my close friends, and family, leaving behind the lifestyle I use to know. I remember the last day I saw my friends. I cried so much that day. Every molecule of water my body could absorb was bursting through my eyes. I felt as though someone took a wrecking ball and flung it through my chest. My pain at that time came from my feelings of great loss. No one died or was going to die; my friends were going to be alive and well. Nonetheless, my pain was as though my friends and family were falling into the abyss, never to be seen again.

This feeling of great loss is experienced by all of us when we get disconnected to the things we love and hold closely to our hearts. Whether it's seeing your only child move away to college, or that sentimental jewelry you have had for 30+ years suddenly disappear, we as humans go through a grieving process for the things and people we are attached to.

Now here is the thing, the heavy emotions of loss and emptiness we experience when we get disconnected from the things and people we care about, our Father in heaven experience these same emotions when we disconnect and turn our backs on Him. When we decide to pursue evil and abandon righteousness God feels a pain of loss.

You don't believe me? Here is proof, in Genesis 6:5-6, we read:

> ADONAI saw that the people on earth were very wicked, that all the imaginings of their hearts were always of evil only. ADONAI regretted that he had made humankind on the earth; it grieved his heart (*CJB*).

Are you surprised that our all-powerful God cares that much when we go astray? I remember thinking, is God really shattered by our evil actions. God is so great and powerful; He can choose to restart a universe whenever He desires. Why would I matter that much to Him? The more I pondered on that question, the more the analogy of a father and a child rested on my heart.

If you promised your son or daughter a great gift for completing a chore you would feel a sense of disheartenment if you learned that the child did not complete the chore. Kids sometimes think that parents are happy to withhold things, but that's quite the opposite. As a parent you desire to give your child the best. You are actually looking forward to delivering on your promise. It hurts you more to withhold the gift than to give it.

This analogy of a gift from a father to his child mirrors God's relationship with us. God knows what He has created for us to enjoy in eternity. He desires to deliver on His promise. It grieves Him when we run astray and forfeit the prize He has in stored for us. It grieves Him because He knows the end all too well.

No wonder God rejoices when we turn away from destruction and return to Him. Luke 15:7 describes the one lost sheep that returns home: "I tell you that in the same way, there will be more joy in heaven over one sinner who turns to God from his sins than over ninety-nine righteous people who have no need to repent" (*CJB*).

Isn't it amazing to know how much God loves us? It grieves Him when we stray, but His joy is uncontainable when we return to him!

We experience unpleasant emotions when we lose something or

someone that we felt connected to. The emotions and pain experienced in those situations are exemplary of God's feelings towards us when we choose to forsake good for evil. Imagine, God loves us so much that He cares when we go off track. He isn't sitting on his glorious throne waiting for a reason to just zap us as soon as we stray. I think this type of love and care should have meaning to us. We should absorb the fact that God's love for us rings deep, so let's remember that then reciprocate our love to Him by never forsaking His ways.

WEEK 50 | ACTIVITY

God's love for us is so great, therefore, the greatest way to show our gratitude to Him is by staying on His path by following after righteousness and forsaking the ways of the Adversary. What are those things that's causing you to stray from His path of righteousness? Whatever those things are take an active step this week to put them aside. Know that you have the authority to overcome the things that seek to separate you from God's love.

For your journey this week, rather than saying I won't do this "thing" whatever it may be, spin it to focus on the positive "thing" you can do. Through this approach, your mind will be focused on engaging in the good. Here's an example, instead of saying, "I will avoid gossip this week, because this is not what God wants of me", instead say, "I will focus this week on spreading good cheer and words of encouragement every chance I get." Write a series of these positive and reinforcing statements that will get you to overcome the things that have been pulling you to stray from His path of righteousness.

_____

_____

_____

_____

_____

_____

_____

51

"ARE YOU READY YET? YOU ARE KEEPING US BACK FROM ORDERING."

*The Spiritual Message: Let nothing hold you
back from connecting with God.*

I recall one afternoon my daughter, my wife, and I were all playing. During our moment of fun and games we decided to race each other. Without a doubt it was evident I was the fastest after our first round of races. On the next round of races my daughter thought it best to see her mom win, so she threw her weight on my back using every bit of strength she had to pull me backwards as I tried to push forward to win the race.

This experience reminded me of the words written in Romans 8:35: "Who will separate us from the love of the Messiah? Trouble? Hardship? Persecution? Hunger? Poverty? Danger? War?" (*CJB*). Paul's words in Romans 8 are an affirmation to us that God's love for us is held with an unbreakable bond. When we join with the Messiah, all the things of old that sought to break our connection with God becomes powerless. The things of old becomes powerless because we take on the newness of His Spirit which allows us to cement our roles as heirs in the kingdom. The question then is how confident are we that we are heirs? And if not, what are the things that are keeping us back from cementing our place as heirs in His Kingdom?

Isaiah 59:1-3 speaks of somethings that have separated us from God:

> Adonai's arm is not too short to save, nor is his ear too dull to hear. Rather, it is your own crimes that separate you from your God; your sins have hidden his face from you, so that he doesn't hear. For your hands are stained with blood and your fingers with crime; your lips speak lies, your tongues utter wicked things (*CJB*).

The things that separate us from God, a separation that stops the divine intervention we earnestly need, are our own sinful actions. This is where some folks may get the urge to turn the leaf. We never like being told that we are at err, or that the things we are doing are sinful. But this is not about pointing out sins though, what this lesson is about is the ability for us to evaluate ourselves to ensure there is nothing holding us back from experiencing the full love and blessings from God.

One of my favorite characters in the bible is King Josiah. I know, most folks love David, and Elijah and Moses, the usual biblical leaders that both the secular and non-secular community talk about. But King Josiah, to me, is the paragon of ensuring everything is done so that nothing separates you from God. King Josiah's fathers abandoned the ways of God, they took pride in breaking the first and second commandments. They built worthless Asherim and other vessels for Baal, worshipping these gods as their true god. They went as far as encouraging the sacrifices of children to these foreign gods. They did all the evil Adonai forbade upon entering the promised land. But here came King Josiah, he tore his clothes when he learned of all the words written in the Law of God. Notice, he didn't just hear the words of the Law then bowed and said a prayer of repentance. No, he swiftly took action to correct the ways of Judah. He tore down the Asherim and destroyed all the pagan altars. King Josiah identified all the things that were keeping Judah from their blessings. Judah's state of war with the surrounding nations was a direct impact of their crimes, and a direct reason for God staying aloof and neglecting to help.

I fervently believe the actions by King Josiah is the standard for all of us. As soon as we identify the behaviors, thoughts, whatever it may be that is the antithesis of God, we should always act swiftly to tear down and burn those things out of our lives.

So, I ask again, what are the things that are preventing you from cementing your position as heirs in His kingdom? Whatever those things are, don't let them separate you from God so that He hides His face and shorten His hand from intervening on your behalf. Don't miss the opportunity to join with the Son and the Father in the new Jerusalem! What's holding you back?

WEEK 51 | ACTIVITY

Dear Father,
We realize that we live in a world that is filled with distractions that can draw us away from you. May our faith be strengthened, and our heart and mind be guarded from the darts of the enemy that is eagerly waiting to destroy us. Forgive me of any, and all trespasses I have committed against you, whether knowingly or unknowingly. This day forward, may nothing separate me from your love, from your promises, from your blessings towards me.
Amein.

Feel free to say this prayer regularly to the Father. Talk to Him about the mishaps that seems to happen often which are causing you to be drawn away from His paths. Let nothing hold you back or separate you from His love. Look at all parts of your life today, if you identify behaviors, people, situations, or thoughts that seek to separate you from God, then it's time to step away from these variables that are in your life. It may be helpful to jot these detractors down accompanied by the words "No more." Do this as a proclamation to yourself that you will overcome these detractors that are holding you back.

_____

_____

_____

_____

_____

52

"I Think My Card Declined"

*The Spiritual Message: Look past the judgement
of others, you always have value!*

When I was younger and first read the recount of David taking Bathsheba, Uriah's wife, I felt great anger learning he executed such a vile act upon an innocent and loyal man. For years I never understood how a person that had the opportunity to choose any available Israeli woman would choose a betrothed Bathsheba. What's the lesson in this God? Is it the fact we all need Your forgiveness, no matter who we are? Forgiveness is certainly part of the lesson, but it wasn't until many years later I realized the other lesson. The other lesson in David's sin with Uriah's wife is centered on Yeshua.

All things started through Yeshua, and end through him, therefore everything that occurs ultimately points to Yeshua. Every scripture we read, directly or indirectly, revealed, or unrevealed, points to the Savior. So, what do I mean? Let's explore further. In the book of Matthew, in the first chapter we read:

The record of the genealogy of Jesus the Messiah, the son of David, the son of Abraham:

> Abraham fathered Isaac, Isaac fathered Jacob, and
> Jacob fathered Judah and his brothers. Judah fathered
> Perez and Zerah by Tamar, Perez fathered Hezron, and

Hezron fathered Ram. Ram fathered Amminadab, Amminadab fathered Nahshon, and Nahshon fathered Salmon. Salmon fathered Boaz by Rahab, Boaz fathered Obed by Ruth, and Obed fathered Jesse. Jesse fathered David the king. David fathered Solomon by her *who had been the wife* of Uriah. Solomon fathered Rehoboam, Rehoboam fathered Abijah, and Abijah fathered Asa. Asa fathered Jehoshaphat, Jehoshaphat fathered Joram, and Joram fathered Uzziah (*NASB*, Matt. 1.1-8).

Right there, six verses in, we see that Yeshua, the one who came to save us from the penalties of sin, came from a genealogy where a guy committed grave sins in the form of adultery and murder. Wow! I still remember the first time I read and absorbed Matthew 1. I felt such great remorse in my spirit as I discovered the true testimony of Yeshua. Here I was pondering and trying to relate to the experience between David and Uriah, but I did not fully understand that Yeshua purposefully allowed these experiences to occur so we all can identify with him!

Many of us don't have access to the country club or send our kids to private schools that equal the cost of a college tuition. When we happen to be amid such people who dress differently, drive different cars, and have a completely different lifestyle, their experiences and conversations feel unrelatable to us. I believe that type of disconnect is what Yeshua wanted to ensure humanity didn't feel with him. Our value, our purpose, isn't tied to our past mistakes, shortcomings, or tumultuous experiences. We have greater value in Yeshua who has delivered us from sin. Yeshua is presenting us as blameless sons and daughters.

God purposefully laid out a genealogy leading up to Yeshua filled with highs and lows so we all can connect to the impeccable being that provided our salvation. In Matthew chapter 1, just looking at the characters in the first seven verses, there's such an intense history of trials and shortcomings that most of us can connect with in some way.

Think about it, Abraham left his home to be a sojourner. Abraham then went from settling with the thought that he will never have a child, to then being the father of nations. Jacob was constantly taken advantage of by his father-in law. Jacob went from being taken advantage of to having a great economical advantage with insurmountable flocks, herds and land. Rahab regarded with low value as a prostitute in her land, became the primary military success strategy in helping Israel conquer Jericho. And David, despite his shortcomings of adultery and murder, he was regarded as a man after God's own heart!

I will close with these words: I know your life experiences are no different than the individuals listed in Matthew 1. Their lives were filled with shortcomings, errs, trials, unfairness, you name it. You have had the same experiences. But what is clear is that despite others may hold these experiences against you, holding you in low regard, remember that God holds you in high regard. I have learned that lesson. Like David, my missteps are just that, they are temporary steps off the right path. Therefore, once we can be humble enough to bow and truly repent, our Father will forgive us. God's forgiveness reassures us that the path ahead holds great value and promise beyond our yesterday.

WEEK 52 | ACTIVITY

List the past experiences you are holding on to that makes you feel less than. After writing those things down, go ahead and strikethrough every one of them. More than a physical exercise, when striking through each one, take the time to appreciate that a strikethrough for each one is like a strike through from God. He has placed it all into the sea of forgetfulness, forgetting your past. God desires a great future for you, a future that is more valuable than your past.

In your quiet moments of prayer, also pray for Yeshua's help to release the burdens of the past which have been keeping you captive from the value you have to offer this world.

> *Dear Father,*
> *Under the authority of Yeshua, I come before you. I desperately need your help. Sometimes I feel as though I am past forgiveness. Sometimes I feel like I have no value. But help me to remember the examples of David, and Rahab, and others of ancient days. Despite their sins and flaws, you Mighty God, used these individuals to carry out majestic works in this world. So today, please send your Spirit to remind me that you are not done with me yet. Help me to realize I am your valuable vessel with a future brighter than my past.*
> *Amein.*

_____

_____

_____

_____

_____

BIBLIOGRAPHY

"5 Greek & Hebrew Words for Love." Olive Tree Blog, 2020, www.olivetree.com/blog/5-greek-hebrew-words-love/Day/.

Aubrey, Allison. "Bad Diets Are Responsible For More Deaths Than Smoking, Global Study Finds." *NPR*, 3 Apr. 2019, www.npr.org/sections/thesalt/2019/04/03/709507504/bad-diets-are-responsible-for-more-deaths-than-smoking-global-study-finds.

Benner, Jeff. "Learn the Ancient Pictographic Hebrew Script." Ancient Hebrew Research Center, 2020, www.ancient-hebrew.org/learn/learn-the-ancient-pictographic-hebrew-script.htm.

Benner, Jeff. "Worship." Ancient Hebrew Research Center, 2020, www.ancient-hebrew.org/definition/worship.htm.

Britannica, The Editors of Encyclopedia. "Jehoiakim". Encyclopedia Britannica, 30 Dec. 2019, https://www.britannica.com/biography/Jehoiakim.

Britannica, The Editors of Encyclopedia. "Acts of the Apostles." Encyclopedia Britannica, 18 Aug. 2020, https://www.britannica.com/topic/The-Acts-of-the-Apostles-New-Testament.

Butler, Trent C. Editor "Gall." StudyLight.org, 1991, www.studylight.org/dictionaries/hbd/g/gall.html.

Chaim Bentorah. "Word Study – Rejoice With Trembling." Chaim Bentorah, 18 Aug 2014, www.chaimbentorah.com/2014/08/word-study-rejoice-trembling/.

"Chanak – A Tool for Discipleship." The Source, 01 Feb. 2019, https://theresource.org.uk/chanak-a-tool-for-discipleship/.

Cherry, Kendra. "Stages of Prenatal Development." Verywellmind, 2020, https://www.verywellmind.com/stages-of-prenatal-development-2795073

Ciampanelli, Paul. "Nature' Most Peaceful Animals." Mom.com, 2020, www.mom.com/momlife/19062-natures-most-peaceful-animals/doves.

"Current World Population." Worldometer, 2020, https://www.worldometers.info/world-population/

Dail, Kan. "Top 10 Calmest Animals In The World." Feri.org, 2019, www.feri.org/calmest-animals-in-the-world/.

"Death Toll From The Slave Trade." World Future Fund, 2020, www.worldfuturefund.org/Reports/Slavedeathtoll/slaverydeathtoll.html

Eisenstein, Lena. "What Is a Vision Statement and Why Is It Important." BoardEffect, 29 Nov. 2019, www.boardeffect.com/blog/what-vision-statement-why-important/

Encyclopedia Judaica, The Editors of Encyclopedia, "Poison." Jewish Virtual Library, 2020, www.jewishvirtuallibrary.org/poison

"Envy." Bible Study Tools, 2020, https://www.biblestudytools.com/dictionary/envy/.

Gallagher, Kisha. "Hebrew Numbers 1-10." Grace in Torah, 15 Jun. 2015, www.graceintorah.net/2015/06/15/hebrew-numbers-1-10/.

Genard, Gary. "10 Causes of Speech Anxiety that Create Fear of Public Speaking." Genard Method, 28 Apr. 2019, www.genardmethod.com/blog/bid/169656/top-10-causes-of-speech-anxiety-that-create-fear-of-public-speaking.

"Gossip, Rumors and Lashon Hara (Evil Speech)." My Jewish Learning, 2020, www.myjewishlearning.com/article/gossip-rumors-and-lashon-hara-evil-speech/

"Grief." Dictionary APA, 2020, https://dictionary.apa.org/grief

Hall-Flavin M.D., Daniel. "Clinical depression: What does that mean?" Mayo Clinic, 2020, www.mayoclinic.org/diseases-conditions/depression/expert-answers/clinical-depression/faq-20057770.

"Hanak." Abarim Publications Biblical Dictionary, 2020, //www.abarim-publications.com/Dictionary/ht/ht-n-kfin.html

Isaminger, Marilyn. "Tending Doves: Peace for Your Home." Herlife Magazine, 2020, www.herlifemagazine.com/blog/pets-for-people/tending-doves-peace-for-your-home/.

"It Rains On the Just and the Unjust, Doesn't Mean What You Think." Deeper Believer, 19 Jun. 2020, https://deepbeliever.com/it-rains-on-the-just-and-the-unjust-doesnt-mean-what-you-think/

"Jealousy vs. Envy: Differences between Envy vs Jealousy." 7ESL, 2020, https://7esl.com/jealousy-vs-envy/.

Khoury, Peter. "7 Unbelievable Fear of Public Speaking Statistics." Magnetic Speaking, 2020, www.magneticspeaking.com/7-unbelievable-fear-of-public-speaking-statistics/.

Lees, Monique. "Statupedia: What Does Stealth Mean?", Startup Institute, 2020, www.startupinstitute.com/blog/2015-05-05-what-is-stealth-mode.

Lin, Ruoyun., Van de ven, Niels., Utz, Sonja. "What triggers envy on Social Network Sites? A comparison between shared experiential and material purchases." Computers in Human Behavior, Aug. 2018, https://www.ncbi.nlm.nih.gov/pmc/articles/PMC5990704/.

McLeod, Saul. "Maslow's Hierarchy of Needs." Simply Psychology, 29 Dec. 2020, www.simplypsychology.org/maslow.html

"Mercy." Jerusalem Prayer Team, 2020, https://hebrew.jerusalemprayerteam.org/mercy-compassion-womb/.

Murphy, John. "7 health dangers aggravated by stress." MDLinx, 11 Jun. 2020, www.mdlinx.com/article/7-health-dangers-aggravated-by-stress/5MRhVjD6ZY9cNTGjucJDT5.

Orr, James, M.A., D.D. General Editor. "Entry for 'HOURS OF PRAYER'". "International Standard Bible Encyclopedia". 1915.

Paige, G. "The Mind's Eye." Data Driven Investor, 2020, www. medium. datadriveninvestor.com/the-minds-eye-825dfc2e5268

"Perception of Authority." SafeHome.org, 31 Jun. 2021, www.safehome.org/perception-of-authority/.

"Perfection." Merriam-Webster.com Dictionary, Merriam-Webster, https://www.merriam-webster.com/dictionary/perfection.

Peterson-More, Diana. "'Be Brief, Be Brilliant, Be Gone." Maximizing Communication - Diana Peterson - More, 11 Dec. 2019, https://dianapetersonmore.com/2019/12/11/be-brief-be-brilliant-be-gone-maximizing-communication/.

Power, Rhett. "A Day of Rest: 12 Scientific Reasons It Works." Inc. Magazine, 17 Jan. 2017, www.inc.com/rhett-power/a-day-of-rest-12-scientific-reasons-it-works.html.

"Rebellion." KJV Dictionary, 2020, https://av1611.com/kjbp/kjv-dictionary/rebellion.html.

"SMART Goals." MindTools, 2020, www.mindtools.com/pages/article/smart-goals.htm.

The Mysterious World, The Editors of The Mysterious World. "Top 10 Most Aggressive Animals In The World." The Mysterious World, 2020, https://themysteriousworld.com/most-aggressive-animals/

"Unhealthy eating and physical inactivity are leading causes of death in the US." Center For Science In The Public Interest, 2020, www.cspinet.org/eating-healthy/why-good-nutrition-important.

"Why Do We Fear Public Speaking?" Quantified, 25 Jul. 2013, www.quantified communications.com/blog/why-do-we-fear-public-speaking/

Wiener, Rabbi Nancy. "Text Study: Cities of Refuge." T'ruah: The Rabbinc Call for Human Rights, 2020, www.truah.org/wp-content/uploads/MIH/ MIH-117-122-text-study-cities-refuge.pdf

Zondervan Academic, The Editors of Zondervan Academic. "When Was Acts Written." Zondervan Academic, 12 Jan. 2018, https://zondervanacademic.com/ blog/when-was-acts-written